A Second Chance to Say Goodbye

A Bridge to the Other Side

Marianne Michaels
with Anita Curtis

Copyright © 2002, 2021 by Marianne Michaels
All rights reserved

No part of this book may be reproduced or transmitted in any form whatsoever without prior written permission from the publisher except in the case of brief quotations embodied in critical articles and reviews.

ISBN 978-1-7340654-3-5 Paperback

Second Edition

Library of Congress Control Number: 2021911414

The information in this book is offered without guarantee on the part of the author or Lunar Light Press. The author and Lunar Light Press disclaim all liability in connection with the use of this book.

Front Cover Image by Shutterstock

Printed in the United States of America
by 48 Hour Books

Published by Lunar Light Press
Bethlehem, PA

I dedicate this book to my Dad,
my brother, Neil,
my dear friend Fran,
Anita's husband, Vic,
and to my angel Heik
who watches over me.
I also dedicate this book to all
the spirits who want to be heard.
It is because of them I do this work.

Contents

Acknowledgments..ix
Preface..xi
Introduction..xv
PART ONE Finding My Purpose..................................1
  CHAPTER 1   The Long Journey Home................3
PART TWO Second Chances......................................41
  CHAPTER 2   "If I Had Only Said Goodbye"....43
  CHAPTER 3   Terminal Illness.........................51
  CHAPTER 4   Abrupt Illness...........................63
  CHAPTER 5   Sudden Death.............................71
  CHAPTER 6   Suicide..................................81
  CHAPTER 7   Murder...................................95
  CHAPTER 8   Animals and the Afterlife..........125
PART THREE Receiving Peace..................................135
  CHAPTER 9   Glimpses of the Other Side........137
  CHAPTER 10 Transforming Grief into
                    Peace..................................145

CHAPTER 11	How Children Grieve..................155
CHAPTER 12	Connecting with Your Loved One..................................167
CHAPTER 13	Communicating Through Meditations............................179
CHAPTER 14	Dream Visitations.......................189
CHAPTER 15	My Second Chance to Say Goodbye......................................197

About the Authors...203
Other Works by Marianne...205

Acknowledgments

I would like to thank my husband, Lucas, for helping me on my journey. And my children, Sarah and Marcus, for giving me an occasional quiet time to write this book. A loving thanks to my mother who awakened me to the spirit world.

Special thanks to my dear friend Anita Curtis who always believed in me and for her patience with all the long hours it took to write this book.

A heartfelt thanks to Jodee Blanco for being my angel that walks on Earth.

A warm thanks to Antonia Felix for her brilliant work that has truly made my words flow. Clair Gerus for her vision of this book. Barbara Haines Howett for forcing me to put my thoughts down on paper. Phyllis Rice, Judy Zysk, Barbara Roboratti and Susan Ajamian for their sharp eyes.

A grateful thanks to Suzane Northrup, my teacher, who fine-tuned my gift. Also to my elder teacher Sophie Bloomfield who grounded me.

I was so fortunate to have my students who were there for me through the years it took to write this book. Teaching them allowed me to grow.

A mindful thanks for Thich Nhat Hanh, my spiritual teacher, who has taught me to find peace in the moment.

A special thanks to all my friends and family for being a part of my life.

My deepest gratitude to my clients who shared their stories and so freely gave of their hearts. And to their loved ones who have crossed over for sharing their messages with me. Without them my work would not be possible.

For the second edition: I would like to thank Barbara Cohen for bringing the need for this edition to my attention and Joan Downing for her creative skills that made this book a reality.

Preface

In 2002, I published my first book, *A Second Chance to Say Goodbye*. I was able to find guidance and gather information with the help of the spirit world. Through the years so much has changed, yet the message of this book remains the same.

In twenty years, my life has changed in many ways. I was divorced and raised two wonderful children as a single mother. I took care of my mother as her health declined, and I sat by her bedside as she died. What has stayed the same is my dedication to Spirit. My path is to teach the understanding that there is no death and to heal those who are grieving. The soul and the connection you share with those you love does not die. As a medium, I have sat at the bedside of the dying and been privileged to watch the celebration of the world beyond as the soul rises in love and light and then is embraced by his or her spirit family.

Recently, I took a trip to North Carolina to drop my son off at college. While there, I took a few days to sit by the water and enjoy the warmer weather. My friend Barbara had been urging me to re-read *A Second Chance To Say Goodbye* with the hope that I would release a second edition. Because of the suffering in this world, she felt its information was once again needed. This was the perfect time to re-read my book. By the time I finished reading it, I realized Barbara was right.

I sat and reflected on the world around me, a world that is caught in a pandemic with death all around us. The fear of death and the fear of losing a loved one and never getting the chance to say goodbye are overwhelming us. Although I felt that I needed to update parts of the book, I realized that the message of this book is needed more than ever.

If you have been fortunate to sit by the bedside of your loved one and watch her transition into the light, know that she knew you were next to her and heard your goodbyes. If goodbyes could not be said, know they were understood. For those who were not with their loved one at the time of death, whether because of a sudden death or visitation restrictions, know your loved one was not alone. The spirits of their loved ones were there to help in the transition and lead their souls into the light.

During the pandemic I have spoken to many people whose loved one was quarantined at the moment of death. Their guilt was overwhelming because they imagined that their loved one had died alone. But when

I listened to the stories told by the spirits, there was a common thread. The one who was dying was never alone. Someone sat with them. Whether it was a deceased spouse, parent or child, someone was there. It was also very common that the spirit of a pet sat close, waiting for the last breath. When the last breath came, the spirit was set free, and a blanket of love was sent from above to those left behind to grieve. During my sessions I help my clients feel this blanket of love, and in this book I will give you the tools and the understanding to also feel this connection.

The message of this book remains the same: "Death is the end of a life but not of a relationship." The relationship between souls does not die but instead continues through time and space. I share the second edition of this book with you with an open heart, with my deepest hope that you can truly have your second chance to say goodbye.

Marianne Michaels
March 24, 2021

Introduction

As a child I would go to my bedroom and sit quietly to wait for visits from spirits. At first I did not know who they were, but their visits felt completely natural and did not frighten me. I described these visitors to my mother, and she recognized them as family members who had passed on. She acted as if this was quite normal, so I never thought much of it. It was like having any other guest drop by. I am convinced that many children see spirits but are told by their parents that it is simply their imagination. This attitude teaches them to ignore the visits. Most of my mother's family experienced psychic events at one time or another, so it was a comfortable topic that could be discussed easily around our house. Therefore, I did not shut myself off to the spirits, and they continued to talk to me because I continued to listen.

I was quite apprehensive about writing this book. My spiritual path hasn't been straight and narrow but filled with detours and almost insurmountable roadblocks. My guides and angels stayed with me in spite of my choices. As you will learn in Chapter 1, these choices included working in New York City's clubs and becoming the mistress of a Mob figure when I was in my early twenties. My solid connection to my spirit guides never left me, however, even when I turned away and refused to listen to them. They threw many opportunities in my path, some of which I ignored and some which I took to heart. Eventually, I reconnected fully with my spirit, accepted my psychic gifts and took responsibility for them. As a result my life took on an enriching new purpose of helping others find peace over the death of a loved one and form a new bond of love and communication.

A Second Chance to Say Goodbye offers advice on how to say goodbye to the old relationship, the relationship you once knew when your loved one was alive. Even though the soul has moved into a different dimension, communication can still be made. You will learn how to connect with the soul of your loved one once you understand the needs of the soul. A new relationship will develop as you learn to raise your vibrations through meditation.

A Second Chance to Say Goodbye is for those who are grieving. Stories taken from sessions with dozens of my clients reveal what happens after the death of the body when the soul makes the transition to a new life. Not only does the soul live on, but it also has a job to do in the heavenly realm. With an understanding of this process and a commitment to quieting your mind in meditation, you can develop contact with the other side and create a new relationship with your loved one, tuning in to the eternal bond that has always been there.

It is my hope that this book will give those who grieve a second chance to say goodbye and make peace with a loved one. It will help you learn there is a bridge to the other side that you can cross to reach peace and understanding. It will also show you that the loved one who passed may also need a chance to say goodbye.

A Second Chance to Say Goodbye is also for those who are suffering the anticipation of grief because a loved one is getting ready to make his final transformation. It will show you how to prepare for the inevitable event to come and enable you to help your loved one understand that death. I've observed this to be a powerful experience that helps the dying lose their fear of going to an unknown place and pass to the next life in peace. Hand in hand, you can make the journey a loving moment for everyone involved.

When I began writing this book, I did not want to reveal my past for all the world to see, but my guides were adamant. They told me that I had to let people know that we can return to our spiritual path no matter how far we have strayed, and I was certainly a good example. When I spoke to my clients to discuss their stories, I felt the pain they had experienced in their grief and knew there was a need for this book. Everyone needs to understand death because when it touches your life, you realize how fragile you are. With preparation and understanding, you can transform bitter loss into a deeper bond of love.

Part One of *A Second Chance to Say Goodbye* is my story. I share how the death of my older brother when I was very young and the anger and confusion that followed turned me away from the spirit world. Not until I was an adult would I be compelled out of loneliness to reconnect with my angels and guides and discover my purpose for being here. I'm not proud of the things I did, but being the rebel I am, I chose to wake up to truth through pain. I had to look my ego in the face in order to let it go and therefore learn to love unconditionally and be accepting of others. I had to realize how lucky I was to be in the physical body and how it is my right to be truly happy. My story is also about the day I watched my father die—the day I realized that I really have no control over life. There is a higher force with a higher plan. I now give thanks every day for having been guided to find the balance inside myself that allows me to do this work.

In Part Two, I share stories from my clients that reveal how the different situations that cause death such as terminal illness, suicide, abrupt illness and murder have different meanings to the soul. The experiences in this section portray how the soul is guided to find peace in the aftermath of physical pain and suffering and how those who are left behind can also find peace from messages that only the departed can offer. For example: The thousands of souls who chose to leave their physical bodies during the horrific attack on the World Trade Center are now at peace in the afterlife. However, their loved ones are left behind to deal with their grief and unanswered questions.

The third part of *A Second Chance to Say Goodbye* contains methods for making the new bond of love and communication with the departed. As the case examples show, anyone can develop this gift and learn how to build upon the love that was once enjoyed while your loved one walked this Earth. This section answers many questions about the unknown and teaches you methods for traveling to the heavenly realm through meditation.

Feelings of loss will always be in the heart of those who grieve. I understand that the change that has come into your life has caused you unbearable pain. Working through the stages of grief can bring you to acceptance. The affirmations and meditations offered in this section can transform your pain into healing, freeing your soul to walk the path you were born to take. You will learn how to see, hear and feel signs from your loved one on the other side. You will then learn how to move forward into a new, soul-to-soul relationship.

I am fortunate that, through my gifts, I have been able to provide comfort to those on this side who needed to say goodbye to the old relationship. Part of this gift is the ability to hear messages from those on the other side that are sent to friends and family. My guides let me know that I was to share what I had learned and to teach others that communication is possible.

My guides were clear about the importance of the third part of this book. We are all able to communicate with the other side, and I hope this section will help you enhance your abilities. I was fortunate that my mother was so matter-of-fact about talking to spirits when I was very young, but I had to spend long periods of time studying with teachers whom I trusted to help me develop my gift.

In my sessions and workshops, I receive much joy when my clients find their way through grief. It is my deepest hope that this book will strengthen your faith and bring you to an understanding to help you heal your heart.

PART ONE

Finding My Purpose

*There is a land of the living
and a land of the dead
and the bridge is love,
the only survival,
and the only meaning.*

—Thornton Wilder

CHAPTER 1

The Long Journey Home

When my mother was thirteen, she began having a recurrent dream that always began the same way. She was standing with her three children on a cliff overlooking the water. Bubbles came to the surface, and she knew that one of her children had drowned, but she couldn't identify which one. In the dream she was helpless to save the child because she couldn't swim. She would wake up in a sweat, shaking with anxiety.

The dream continued after she was married and had a family, but as there were only two children, she didn't pay much attention to it. Then came the surprise. Me. I was born when she was forty-two, and her dream became more threatening. It also became more frequent. My mother was extremely fearful whenever any of us were near the water.

One day when I was five years old, I was sitting in my favorite oak tree. The wind was blowing against my face, and I could smell the fragrance of lilacs. All was right in my little world, so I was totally unprepared for the disruption that was about to happen. My twenty-three year old brother, Neil, was coming to cook lunch, and I hoped he would make my favorite—potatoes and eggs. I also hoped he would bring along his seventeen-year old wife, Grace, who was five months pregnant. I loved her and was thrilled with the idea of being an aunt.

That morning, my twenty-year-old sister, Lucille, was planning to go out with her friends. As she started to get into the car, my mother ran out of the house screaming, "Neil's been in an accident! He's missing! You have to take me to Morgan's Creek!"

Apparently, Neil had been practicing for a big boat race in New Jersey's Morgan's Creek. The Coast Guard had called to say there had been an accident, and Neil was missing. My father took the call and drove off to the search site without saying a word to my mother. He knew Mom would be hysterical, and he couldn't deal with her as well as the tragedy of possibly losing his son.

My mother had overheard part of the call, specifically the words "accident" and "missing." She knew at once that it was about Neil. Then she started to cry out, "I didn't get a chance to say goodbye!" She screamed it over and over, and as I listened from my perch in the tree, my wonderful world suddenly fell apart. Those words are still etched in my memory.

A neighbor offered to drive my mother to the creek. When they arrived, my mother walked to the water and stood on the bank looking down. The ebb and flow of the water caused a group of bubbles to float near the bank. When my mother saw them, she knew her worst nightmare had finally materialized. It was everything she had seen in her dream.

The ordeal of the search lasted seven hours. I stayed behind at a neighbor's house but learned the details later. My father, mother and sister endured the deafening sound of helicopters roaming overhead and the horrifying sight of rescue boats slowly moving about. When my father heard that they had found a body, he took my mother into a shed, but my sister could not be moved from her spot. She watched in hope that it wasn't Neil but saw his body and curly black hair as he was being pulled into the rescue boat. That moment was the beginning of the pain that she would have to work through for years and years to come. Her life, like mine, was changed forever.

At the viewing and funeral, I felt confused over everyone's grief. Since talking to spirits was so common in my family and Neil was now a spirit, why did everyone say he was gone? I wondered. I was born into a deeply religious Italian Catholic family, and my mother was devoted to the church. However, our family has always been matter-of-fact about spirits, and nobody questions the stories of spirit encounters that come up at family gatherings. My mother's sister talks to her deceased husband all the time, and nobody in the family finds it unusual. Everyone in the family treats visits from spirits as if they were everyday occurrences.

In my five-year-old mind, I thought it should be okay to be dead. I knew they could still talk to Neil's spirit, but I didn't realize they were mourning the loss of Neil's physical presence. I asked my mother what happened to Neil and why he was lying in the coffin. She told me that he was with God. If he was with God, I couldn't figure out why he was in the coffin. I thought that being with God was supposed to be a good thing. As I looked at the expressions on the faces of the people around me, I tried to understand what made them sad, but it was beyond my comprehension.

Months went by, and Mom continued to scream and cry in agony. No one could comfort her. One night, Neil came to her in a dream and gently told her to stop crying, assuring her that he was okay and reminding her that she needed to take care of her family. After that the uncontrollable screaming stopped, but she continued to cry alone in her bedroom.

Mom's grief was driving her and my father apart. Dad wanted to leave, but at the end of the first year, my mother's body was starting to break down, and she needed radical surgery. I was in a state of panic because I was afraid she would die as Neil had. Thankfully, she recovered, and the birth of Neil's daughter, Carrie, became another blessing to our family. Having part of

Neil with us in the form of his beautiful child helped heal the wound of losing him.

Everyone was so immersed in his or her own grief that no one thought of mine. All the sympathy from friends and family went to my mother and none to my sister or me. Lucille could no longer cope with the sadness that hung over the house, and she and her longtime boyfriend married and left the state. She had been my only link to life, and her leaving made me feel abandoned and angry.

My anger lasted for years and tempered many of my thoughts and actions. I had been seeing spirits all my life, but they stopped appearing to me during the two years after Neil's death, blocked by my strong emotions. One of the last communications I had before the tragedy was the vision of a woman crying in my mother's bedroom. My mother asked me what this spirit looked like, and I described her features and her clothing. This description perfectly matched that of my maternal grandmother whom I had never met because she died before I was born. My mother did not understand why her mother would be crying in her bedroom because at the time life was very happy in our home.

My grandmother had taken care of Neil when he was a young boy and had been very close to him. I believe that her tears in my vision were not over my brother's death but over the heartbreak and pain that my mother would go through. After my brother's death, my mother spent most of her time crying in that room.

By the age of seven, I began to see the spirits again, and once again their presence seemed perfectly normal to me. That year, the spirit of a little boy, who looked to be about six years old, suddenly appeared in front of me. He told me that I would be okay. When I told my mother, she did not react as if the sighting was strange and did not seem the least bit concerned, so I wasn't afraid either. The spirit of the little boy came to me during a time of deep loneliness and need, bringing comfort and acting as my angel and guide. He continued to visit for several years and was a strong healing force in my childhood.

I talked to other children about the spirits, but by the time I was nine years old, they began calling me a witch. I was always around adults at home and did not know how to interact well with other children. I told a girl at school that I was ill and going to die within a year in the hope that she would feel sorry for me and be my friend. It worked, and I finally had a companion my age.

I wasn't popular in high school and never felt like I fit in—until some of my classmates found out I read Tarot cards. Suddenly, they found me unique and interesting, and I enjoyed it. Like most sixteen-year-olds, I was anxious to define my individuality and was confused about how my beliefs and gifts fit into the rest of the world.

My interests were very different from most kids my age, and I just couldn't figure out where I belonged. I felt a strong pull to go to New York City. My soul longed to be there, and I knew something waited for me in that city. The attraction was so strong that I skipped school several times to visit New York, taking the bus from New Jersey and spending the day wandering around. On one occasion I turned a corner and saw a store called The Magical Child. I walked in at once and stayed for hours, talking to the people who worked there and reading books about the spiritual realm. I didn't realize then that the spirits had led me there as part of the preparation for my life journey.

Life took a turn for the better when I met a young man named Joey. He was twenty-three, and I was eighteen and boy-crazy, and we had a very special relationship. At the time I was reading many books on spirituality, and Joey enjoyed listening to me talk about the subject. I bought a pack of Tarot cards at The Magical Child and practiced my readings on him. He was the only male I knew who thought I was interesting rather than weird. I fell deeply and passionately in love.

Even though he was from a wonderful, affluent home, Joey had begun getting into trouble at an early age. I never believed that he used drugs like everyone said he did—until the day I walked into his apartment and found him shooting up heroin. My knees buckled at the sight of him, and I slid down the wall to the floor. He looked like he was dying, and I was terrified that I would lose him, horrified that he would die at the same age as my brother. Joey, meanwhile, was in his own euphoric world. I was devastated but still convinced, deep down, that I could change him. I convinced myself that he would love me even more once I "fixed" him.

Joey's drug use swept me into severe mood swings and depression and, to make it worse, I was having a difficult time at home because my parents disapproved of him. I promised them that I had no desire to try heroin, but they worried.

Sneaking out to spend time with Joey made me frustrated and more depressed. I begged my mother to send me to a psychiatrist to help with my depression, and she finally consented. Unfortunately, at my first session the doctor told me that my problem was sexual inhibition and that if I took my shirt off in his office, I would be cured. I kept my shirt on, picked up my purse and left. Men were obviously everything my mother said they were, I thought, as I walked out the building.

Shortly after I graduated from high school, my mother became a born-again Christian and decided that my interest in the occult was the result of my being possessed by the devil. Not only did she talk about her new-found religious zeal and the sad state of my soul, she acted on it. One morning when I was eighteen years old, she and my aunt rushed at me and threw me on the floor. "We're going to exorcise that demon out of you," my mother said as they held me down and thrust a crucifix in my face. "Kiss it!" they yelled, struggling to open a bottle of holy oil. Kicking and screaming, I was struck by the cross and smeared with oil before I managed to rip myself free and run out of the house. I ran down the street, barefoot and wearing only my nightshirt and shorts, and made my way to Joey's house. My mother had suddenly turned into a lunatic and total stranger, and I felt I had nowhere else to turn. I was lonely and frightened, exhausted by the ordeal as well as by the looming void I felt inside.

Joey answered his door, and I fell into his arms, sobbing. He took me by the hand and led me out to the nearby boardwalk along the beach as I told him what had happened. We strolled along the grounds and got on the Ferris wheel, ascending high into the sky and hovering at the top. Looking down over the ocean, I felt far removed from the world and safe in Joey's arms. He looked at me and said, "Everything is out there waiting for you, Marianne. Don't settle for less. Don't be like me." His words cleared the chaos from my head and made me feel that life was simple and full of hope. I felt free on that Ferris wheel, and I knew no one could get me because Joey wouldn't let anyone hurt me.

A few days later, I was doing a Tarot card reading and drew the card that represented imprisonment. A cold chill went down my back as the image of Joey being arrested flashed in my mind. I told him of the vision and made him promise me that he would stay out of trouble.

The next day the police came to question Joey about a robbery. On my finger they saw the opal ring that Joey had given me as a gift and recognized it from photos of the stolen property in question. They arrested Joey for robbery, and between the ring and the statement of his partner in crime, he was convicted and sentenced to five to seven years in prison. Still in love and still hoping I could change him, I visited often and wrote him letters. But Joey had decided to end our relationship and made it very clear in one of his letters. "You can't be in love with me," he wrote. "I'm no good. You have your whole life ahead of you. I can't give you the things that are important because I don't care about them." He added that he was still in love with his old girlfriend and ended the letter by saying that he would take me off the prison visiting list.

I crushed the letter in my hand and felt the heat of anger rush to my face. Burning with feelings of abandonment and betrayal, I vowed that no one else would ever leave me. This time I would be the one to leave.

With calm and purpose, true to my flair for drama, I sat in my bedroom and swallowed twenty-six barbiturates. If all went as planned, they would find my body at the beach only a few minutes from my parents' house. I figured it would take about fifteen minutes for the pills to do their job, so after getting the twenty-sixth pill down, I headed for the car.

As I walked out of the house, I met my neighbor's boyfriend. He was swigging from a bottle of whiskey and offered me some. I took a drink to wash away the taste of the pills—and immediately passed out.

When I woke up, I looked around and wondered if I had done it. Was this heaven? It didn't appear to be. I didn't believe in hell, so I wasn't sure where I was. Then

I saw the familiar overbed table, chair and white cotton curtain. It was a hospital room. My throat was burning from a tube that had been used to pump my stomach. I turned my head and looked into the face of a doctor who was peering intently at me. I grabbed a box of tissues off the tray by my bed and threw it at him, sending him out of the room. No, this definitely wasn't heaven.

My father came to see me, and he cried. This surprised me because I had no idea how deeply he cared. My father was a man of few words, and I was so involved in my own anger that I never thought of the impact my actions would have on anyone else. My mother knew better than to come to see me. Her heart was breaking, but she knew I didn't want her there.

Even though my mother lived for me and was overprotective out of the fear of losing another child, I was now an embarrassment to her. The law in New Jersey required people who attempted suicide to go to a state mental hospital. My family pulled strings and had me admitted to a private hospital. It sounded like a nice vacation—people waiting on me, lounging in bed, no cooking or cleaning—so I readily agreed to go. I was sedated until I was admitted to the new hospital, and when I arrived, I put my pajamas on and got into bed. Maybe this wasn't a beach in the Caribbean, but I was going to take advantage of the situation as much as possible. I needed time to sort things out, I told myself as I stretched out and put my hands behind my head. A nurse came into the room and demanded to know what

I was doing. I yawned and told her I was going to take a nap. "Patients here dress in street clothes and go to therapy during the day," she said. "You can sleep at night like everybody else." So much for the vacation.

Still a bit groggy, I got dressed and made my way to the recreation room. The scene before me snapped me back to reality. Over by the window stood a woman whose picture I had seen in the newspaper, a maniac who had killed her two children. In a folding chair by the door, another woman, convinced that she was pregnant, screamed with labor pains. This place is full of crazy people! I said to myself. I don't belong with people this sick; I had only tried to commit suicide.

This was not the restful resort scene I had expected, and I decided that instant to get out. Striding down the hall toward the front exit, I was snatched up by two orderlies and taken to my room. They tied me to my bed and gave me a shot of Thorazine. This is all wrong, I said to myself. Maybe there is a hell after all, I thought as I slipped away into a drugged sleep.

The next day I was taken back to the recreation room, but this time I didn't stop to check out the other patients. I crept to the corner of a couch like a frightened animal, wrapped my arms around my knees and cried. I closed my eyes and tried to hear the voice of the little boy angel who had helped me as a child. Nothing. The drugs had made my mind numb. How did I get here? I asked myself. What is wrong with me? How did things get this bad?

Two days later, I met with a doctor for evaluation. I was excited—finally I would be able to talk to someone who would understand me. I started to tell him about the spirits I had seen all my life, but he didn't listen. He was busy shooting off questions from the list in front of him. A spirit's voice came into my head and warned me not to tell him about my gifts, so I stopped talking about the spirits and stuck to answering his questions. The doctor finished his list and said that nothing was wrong with me and that I could go home.

"I don't want to go home," I said.

"All right," he said. "You're a big girl now, so where do you want to go? What would make you happy?"

"New York," I answered.

"So go home, pack, and go," he said.

This was the answer to my prayers, but as soon as I realized I was going to be on my own, I felt a chill of fear.

I went home and thought about the doctor's question of what would make me happy. My answer had been vague. Wouldn't a normal person know at least that much about what they wanted out of life? I thought of Joey. Everyone thought I wanted to kill myself because of Joey, but it was not that simple. The real problem was that I was lost.

In the meantime Joey had been released early from prison and started his life over, sober and drug-free. He asked me to marry him, but I knew he wasn't the answer. For one thing, I had to find my own way without any distractions. For another, Joey had lost something special. Prison had changed him. When we first met, he was a free spirit; but after he got out, his eyes were lifeless and empty. I knew deep in my heart that it was time to let go.

I talked to my parents about my desire to live in New York, but their fear of losing me was so strong that they wouldn't listen. I didn't want to hurt them, but I was twenty years old, and I knew it was time to take control of my life.

I packed my Firebird while my parents were at a prayer meeting and left for New York.

My aunt put me up until I found work as a receptionist in Manhattan and moved into my own tiny apartment. I tried to make peace with my parents and hoped they would understand that I had to live in New York. My father thought I would fail miserably, give up these wild ideas and come home. My mother helped me with extra cash whenever she could, but it was against my father's wishes.

Much to my surprise, I settled in to city life and began to enjoy being on my own. On my birthday just a few weeks into my new job, my friend Lynn came running into the office and set a large box in front of me. I lifted the lid, and a sweet little Siamese cat popped his head up and stared into my eyes. It was love at first sight for both of us. I took the kitten out of the box and held him to me, beginning our twenty-year-long friendship.

Tiki was my favorite companion and friend. One day, sick at home with a cold, I heard him make a strange growl. It was a loud, primordial sound that I didn't even know a domestic cat could make, let alone my gentle little Tiki. I got out of bed and saw him staring toward the window by the fire escape. When I followed his stare, I saw a young man trying to raise my window enough to climb in. I screamed at the top of my lungs, and the man ran off. There had been several rapes in my apartment building, and when the rapist was finally caught, I learned he was the same person who had tried to break in.

This ordeal convinced me that my guides were protecting me, but I was determined to push them out of my life until I could figure out exactly where they fit.

After one year I got fired from my job. I had been unhappy working in an office and was always calling in sick, so it wasn't a big surprise. The rents in New York were so high that I spent almost all of my money keeping a roof over my head. Tiki and I had grown accustomed to macaroni and cheese which was all I could afford most of the time, and I often yearned for the fresh cantaloupes and melons I passed in the vegetable stands. But after I lost my job, I needed every dime for bus fare as I searched for a new job.

My first success came when I signed on with a modeling agency, but the work was sporadic. One day, one of the girls in the agency told me about a job that paid good money with no phones or typing involved. The job was as a hostess in a topless bar. I wasn't sure I wanted to work in a place like that, but as a hostess I could keep my clothes on.

I decided to check it out but spent the good part of an afternoon walking around the block while I thought it over. I couldn't, wouldn't go into that awful place, I said to myself. It wasn't me or who I wanted to be. But I wanted to keep my apartment and be independent. I was in New York, and I wanted to make it.

Somehow I got myself through the door and entered a world of psychedelic lighting, pornography-covered walls, leering men, bumping-and-grinding girls, cocaine and alcohol. I didn't listen to my common sense or my guides but stayed and let my eyes adjust to the dim lights. From that day on, I began a new lifestyle as a creature of the night. One day I would look back and realize that I had entered another level of hell. The hospital was bad enough, but this time I descended into a dark corner fully aware of what lay before me. There is no other hell than the one we make for ourselves here on Earth.

I had pushed my spiritual life aside, refusing to think about or see the spirits that had surrounded me most of my life. When I drank, however, I inadvertently let my guard down and received visitations. One morning as I was waking up, I saw the spirit of a young boy come out of my closet. He put his hand in mine. His face was burnt, scarred and deformed. I could smell smoke around him. I felt fear welling up inside me. I shook my head to make him go away. I found out later that years before I moved in, there had been a fire in the building, and a young boy had died. He panicked in the fire and ran into a closet where he died from smoke inhalation, after which his small body was badly burned.

I may have tried to push away my spiritual side, but it did not give up on me. My heart began to soften, and I developed a new attitude at the bar. I started feeling sorry for the men I talked to and saw them as lost souls who needed help. Much to my surprise, my overall negative view of men changed. Not having dated anyone since Joey, I decided to give men another chance and began to go out with Charlie, the 5' 11', blue-eyed, handsome bouncer at the club. He was smart and efficient and eventually moved up to become a manager. Charlie was self-assured and funny, and our first six months together were great. But eventually, he started to brood and became obsessively jealous. I was not the type to date more than one man at a time, but Charlie didn't believe that. I quit my job at the topless club, but he still accused me of cheating on him. More than once, he flew into a jealous rage and threatened to cut my face or kill my cat. Boy, can I pick them, I thought. Even my cat had better taste in men. He hated Charlie and hid whenever he came into the apartment.

Thankfully, the spirits never left my side and helped me when I least expected it. Charlie had gotten me another job in an illegal gambling club, and one night the club closed early because they suspected there would be a raid. I was waiting for the bus in the freezing night air. The bus pulled up, the driver opened the door, and before I could get in, he said, "The bus is full." The door closed in my face, and the bus pulled away. I could see that the bus was not full, and I was furious. How dare that idiot bus driver tell me there was no room for me on the bus!

I stood in the cold for another half hour waiting for the next bus, fuming and mumbling to myself about what I would like to do to that driver if I ever had a chance. The bus finally arrived, and I fell into a seat, crossed my arms and indulged in my bad mood. The nerve of that guy to cut me off like that! It just didn't make sense. I stomped off the bus at my stop and was almost home when the sight of flashing lights interrupted my silent tirade. I saw Charlie standing with a group of policemen and other people. He was not in handcuffs, so I wondered what was going on. I got closer and asked another onlooker what had happened. He told me that about a half hour earlier, a young woman was walking down the street and had been dragged into my apartment building by a man who then tried to rape her. Her screams attracted a taxi driver and Charlie who both came to her rescue.

I felt sick when I realized, had I not missed that first bus, that girl could have been me. I gave silent, heartfelt thanks to whomever had saved me.

My relationship with Charlie was deteriorating. He once trashed my apartment in a drunken rampage, ripping apart the clothes in my closet as Tiki and I hid beneath the bed. As usual, he cried and apologized after he sobered up. Soon after this, he climbed up the fire escape and smashed garbage cans through my window to get into my apartment. At this point I was afraid for my life and knew I had to move and change my job.

Tony, one of the owners of the Mafia-run illegal gambling club where I worked, came to my rescue. He found me an apartment with a doorman so Charlie couldn't get to me and also drove me to and from work every day. I poured my heart out to him about everything. Before long, he left his girlfriend, and we were a couple. Sort of. I hadn't advanced far in the relationship department because this one was flawed from the start. Tony was married. And he was with the Mob.

After months with Tony, I found I had fallen deeply in love with him, and he with me. Tony's marriage was in name only, but his Italian Catholic background prevented him from ever choosing to leave his wife. He was with me during the day, but I wanted him every night. I wanted him on holidays. I wanted to be the center of his life. When his wife became ill and he had to spend more time at home, I grew terribly jealous. I wanted more—I wanted a family, but I knew I could never have one with Tony. He had told me in the beginning that he was totally committed to his family and would never leave them.

For two years I was a mobster's mistress, and my life was a fantasy. I didn't work, I didn't cook and I was driven everywhere I wanted to go. My days began with a workout at the health club followed by an afternoon of shopping in the Fifth Avenue department stores. I loved B. Altman's for clothes and Bergdorf Goodman for their wonderful hat department—I had a full wardrobe of hats to wear during the summer at the racetrack. In the late afternoon I'd go home, fix myself a cocktail and get dressed up to go out to dinner with Tony. We always went out to expensive places like the Oak Room at the Plaza for four-course meals. Tony bought me jewelry and a mink coat and paid for everything from the rent to the manicurist to the groceries.

When we went to dinner, the other women and I always sat with our backs to the door because Tony and his associates never did. When the conversation turned to business, I would get up and go to the bathroom or have a drink at the bar. I wasn't allowed to listen to any shop talk because the less I knew, the safer I was. Tony was twenty-four years older than I and extremely protective of me, so I took the whole Mob scene lightly and was never afraid. When I caught him looking into the rear-view mirror as if we were being followed, I'd joke about it and make him laugh. I was living a dangerous life, but the power he had made me fearless. I was Tony's girl, and no one could touch me.

Everything about Tony's work for the "family" was unspoken, but the evidence was everywhere. One day, he let me borrow his car to drive to Little Italy and get pastries at Ferrara's. When I hit the brakes to make a turn off Canal Street, a pistol flew out from under the seat. I didn't want to touch it, so I simply kicked it back where it came from. Another day, we were having lunch at a coffee shop, and I followed Tony into a back room. Two men were busy punching out fake Rolexes like the ones sold to tourists all over the streets of New

York. Someone always tipped Tony off about a police raid at the gambling club, and several times we sat in a restaurant within view of the building and watched the police rush in.

Because he refused to get a divorce, I was afraid that Tony would leave me, and my fear came out in emotional outbursts that drove him away. He told me that even though he loved me, he had to leave because I needed a husband and children. Then he was gone.

I was on my own again and was desperate to find a job so I could keep my apartment. I took a job as a restaurant hostess at the Vista Hotel in the World Trade Center. After Tony broke up with me, I was so spoiled that I cried every morning while getting ready to go to work. It was humiliating to wait on people as the breakfast hostess in my ridiculous little-Dutch-girl uniform, and at times I was tempted to return to the other lifestyle and take up with someone else. But I never did. Most women who became mistresses of the Mob never left because the men and the money gave them a sense of freedom and security. But in reality, there is little freedom because you are simply someone's possession. When I came to my senses, I was grateful to have stayed away and forged a new life. But it took many years to stop missing the money, the clothes, the trips, the dinners and the non-stop attention. Once you've been treated like a princess, it's hard to punch a time clock.

In a short time I applied for a different position at the hotel, as a cocktail waitress, and got the job. The money and the hours were much better, and I felt that things were looking up. One evening I was having a conversation with a friend in the ladies' room at the hotel when a woman walked over to me. She looked at me and said, "Why are you denying your path? Read Shakti Gawain's book, *Creative Visualization*." I didn't know what she was talking about, but stranger things had happened to me, so I bought the book. As I read the book, I slowly began to realize that I could create my own life.

I was reading the book in the piano bar of the Palace Hotel when I met a man named Abdul, a thirty-five-year-old Arab who owned an oil company in Kuwait. He lived in Paris but often came to New York on business. I forgot about the book and, after six months of seeing Abdul, took off with him to Paris. He was rich beyond my wildest dreams, good looking, very fun to be with, and he cared about me. I wanted this to be a fairy tale come true in which I would live happily ever after. I tried to ignore the feeling in my gut that warned there was something wrong with him. My instincts were right, of course: He started drinking more and more and criticizing me about everything from my clothes to my American ways.

Abdul decided it was time to move forward into the next stage of our relationship which meant introducing me to his family in Saudi. We were to go to Kuwait first so he could take care of some company business, then go on to Saudi. He told me I would need a visa before we left France, so I told him I'd go to the American embassy to get one. That would take too long, according to Abdul, who said he had friends in the Kuwaiti embassy who would streamline things. When we got to the embassy, we bypassed a very long line of people and went into a back room. A man entered and spoke briefly with Abdul in his native language. Then he turned to me and in English asked for my passport. I asked why he needed it, and he told me they were going to take care of the visa. Abdul and the man were quite insistent about getting my passport from me. I knew I could not travel without it.

I looked into my purse and suddenly heard my spirits tell me in a stern voice not to take out the passport. The message was so clear and stern that I had to act on it. I told Abdul that I had left my passport in his apartment and would bring it the next day.

Abdul went back to work, and I began walking to his apartment. The rest of the day unfolded like a bizarre dream with my spirit guides working overtime to bring me to safety. On the way to the apartment, I realized I was being followed. Heart pounding and mind racing, I made it inside and immediately hid my passport inside a box of rice in the kitchen. I walked out to the terrace and looked over the city, trying to find peace of mind in the beautiful view of Parisian rooftops and the towers of Notre Dame in the distance. I glanced up to another terrace and saw a man smiling at me. He asked if I would like to have a drink with him at a familiar local place. The invitation sounded very innocent, but I didn't think it wise to be so impulsive. At the same time something inside me strongly urged me to go. I didn't understand this feeling, but my gut instinct had just saved me from being forced into a trip to Saudi Arabia from which I may never have been able to return, so I felt compelled to listen to it. As I was leaving the hotel with the man, Abdul came around the corner and saw me. He was furious and caused a nasty scene in the street. His pride was demolished, and he insisted that I leave. I went back into the apartment, secretly gathered my passport and threw all my clothes in a suitcase. Three hours later, I was on a plane for New York.

Back home, I realized that I may have turned my back on the spirits, but they had not turned away from me. My guides had stayed in the background and allowed me to make my own choices. They had bailed me out of trouble many times and probably saved my life.

After returning from Paris, I began to feel a gentle yearning for a family of my own. I wanted to have a productive and enriching life surrounded by a loving husband and children. One day while I was walking down the street, I felt a child take my hand and call out, "Mommy." When I looked down, no one was there. The desire to have a husband and family welled up within me again, but I had to tell the little spirit to wait. The time was not yet right.

Now I needed to find some kind of normality in my life. I began classes at the Fashion Institute of Technology, studying for an associates degree in Fashion Buying and Merchandising. Always putting opportunities in my path, my guides led me to a temporary job as a personal shopper at Saks Fifth Avenue. On my way in one morning, I joked with the coat stockroom man about the sign on his desk that read, "Beam me up, Scotty." He said, "Yeah, I talk with a lot of spirits." Then he looked me straight in the eye and said, "You know what I mean." I did.

My job was eliminated, and I was let go, but Rolando became my spiritual teacher. I went on unemployment for six months, and this wonderful gift of time gave me the freedom to spend every day with him. It was a platonic relationship, and we talked constantly about our spirituality. His knowledge seemed endless, and I wanted to absorb every word he spoke.

As I started opening up to my spirituality, the voice of the child that called me "Mommy" returned. I went into meditation and saw a four-year-old girl with long, dark, wavy hair. I had to tell her that she couldn't come into my life yet because I didn't have a husband. The yearning for a stable family life kept rising to the surface of my awareness, and now I could not deny it.

Rolando and I were sitting before a Ouija board in his apartment one evening with candles and crystals all around us. He was one of the only people I ever met who could keep negativity out of this device. I had been reluctant to use it because I knew it attracted lower entities. Rolando reassured me that his spirit guide Sarduke would be there to keep the lower energies away. He explained that spirit guides or angels are powerful energies from the heavenly realm who have the ability to see both our material and spiritual worlds. They help people on their paths because they are worried about the salvation of Earth. I asked what they look like, and he explained that they appear however you want them to appear.

As we worked the Ouija board, I could see a woman through my third eye. I was surprised to see that she resembled me but with wavy hair instead of straight and wearing a long, flowing dress. Her presence became stronger. As the placket moved, I could hear her words in my head—her name was Heik.

I saw a strong man hammering on stone who pushed her aside, saying, "I am the One from the Sun. I have been your guide and protector since you were a child, and now I am tired of carrying you home."

I was beside myself with joy, and Rolando was delighted too. He asked me what the man looked like. I closed my eyes and pictured him once again: Tall and well built; long, black hair; a combination of Polynesian and South American features in his handsome face.

After the One from the Sun spoke to me, Heik grew stronger and identified herself. She asked permission to give me guidance and said she would like to help me for the rest of my life. I was euphoric. I could hardly contain my excitement and pleasure. I had found my angel.

Heik offered more information about spirit guides. She told me that she is light energy. She comes from a place where beings are more evolved than humans and don't need the lessons of Earth anymore. Heik said that people who come to Earth have to learn material lessons about greed, jealousy, hate and destruction. She said that we on Earth are takers and need-oriented and that we feel we have to evolve by pain.

Spirit guides have come to work with us to help evolve our souls. They enjoy the beauty of Earth and can help us learn how to channel their love. I was told that I had more work to do on myself. For starters, she said that if I continued drinking, I would not be able to see her or the One from the Sun any more.

After a few weeks of communicating with the Ouija board, Heik told me to stop using it because she had to lower her vibrations to come through. She said I was ready to move on. The Ouija board was an easy way for me to work, but I gave it up and concentrated on meditation. Within a few weeks I was able to communicate with them while in a meditative state.

When it came time for me to go back to work, my new guide showed me the first of many amazing tricks she had up her sleeve to help me with my day-to-day life. Heik told me to pull my hair back, fasten it with a big black bow and go to Macy's makeup department. I was to go to the counter that sold lipstick in black tubes. I did as she told me but discovered there were many lipsticks in black tubes. Confused and thoroughly ignorant about makeup, I stood at one of the counters and absently looked around. I leaned on the counter for a minute, trying to think of what to do next. A clerk came to me and asked, "Are you here for the job?"

I said, "Yes." I was interviewed for a position selling Chanel cosmetics and was hired at once.

My life was coming into balance between the spiritual realm and the material world, and I was learning to be comfortable with who I am. I was working and independent. I was spending my free time with my guides and creating the life I wanted. It was time for a partner to come into my life, a partner who would understand me, talk to me, love me and share my spirituality.

My father was dying after years of battling heart attacks, diabetes and Parkinson's disease. As his conditioned worsened, my mother and I grew close again. With the fall of her idols, television evangelists Jim and Tammy Faye Bakker, Mom had let go of her born-again ideas and was back to her more expansive, metaphysical beliefs. She was very interested in my work with my guides and in everything I had to say about my spiritual adventures.

I was with my father during his last days. It was difficult to see this strong, silent man suffer. When he finally let go of this life, I felt his soul in the room with me. "Daddy, if you need to go, go to the light," I said. "And if you can, please help me from the other side. Maybe you could even help me find the right partner." I grieved the death of my father and longed even more for a caring man in my life. My mother lost herself in her grief, and at the same time, my friend Rolando moved to Florida. I was lonely but, to my surprise, well able to deal with the loss.

I had given my will over to Jesus whose life I had been studying. Each morning I performed a soul-mate meditation with music in the background, saying, "Jesus, you pick the man for me because I've done such a bad job." I repeated this ritual for eight months. I did not have anybody to talk to about spiritual matters, and although I dated, each new date was worse than the last.

One night, I joined a friend for a drink, and a good-looking man came into the bar. I tried to focus on my friend's conversation, but my attention was drawn to the man. Every time I looked in his direction, I saw him smiling at me.

When I walked to the ladies room, the bartender stopped me and said, "There's Lucas Rivera, Marianne. He's a nice guy. Why don't you talk to him?" I had to smile to myself at the sound of his name because as a teen, I had a crush on Geraldo Rivera. I imagined being married to him and wrote "Marianne Rivera" over and over again in my notebooks. Marianne Rivera, I thought to myself. But it was only a fleeting thought, and I dismissed it at once.

Lucas, it turned out, had just broken up with his girlfriend, and I had just been on the date from hell the night before. Weeks went by before he finally asked me out. He was a fiction writer by night and a reporter at the *Daily News* by day. We both found it amusing that he had worked across the street from my apartment building for five years. We frequented the same pizza parlor, deli and restaurants but had never run into each other. My guides, I learned, did not let me meet him during those years because he had major issues to work out.

Lucas was my friend and eventually became my lover. One evening as we sat together quietly, he suddenly said, "It's you!"

He had had a dream before we met in which a woman, all dressed in white, came into his bedroom. She made love to him, and it was wonderful. Then she was gone, leaving behind only her smile, a sweet aroma and the image of hair flowing down her back. He woke crying because he didn't want it to be over and didn't know where to find her. That evening he realized that I was the woman in his dream. We knew in that moment that we would spend the rest of our lives together. I also had Tiki's approval. When Lucas first met him, he said, "A Siamese cat! I love Siamese cats!"

I felt that my father was smiling down at us because I knew he had wanted to see me settled. One evening, someone—and I believe it was my father—sent a message loud and clear. Lucas and I were having a pleasant evening together at home when the blender in the kitchen suddenly started. Not only was it out of reach, it wasn't even plugged in! I told Lucas then that if he was going to cut and run, this was the time. It must have been love. He stayed with me.

We were together for a year when we decided to get married. We honeymooned in Greece where I was compelled to go to Delos, an island of ruins. I left the tour group to meditate on a hill overlooking the beach, and that powerful experience allowed me to hear sounds of the people who once thrived on the now-desolate island. At one time Cleopatra used this island to meet both Marc Anthony and Caesar. I knew I had been there in a previous lifetime, but I couldn't remember anything about it. I knew the detours of my early life were behind me and that I was solidly on my path now, but I had no idea where that path led. I just knew I had to stay on it. I meditated and asked that it be revealed to me, but there was no answer.

On the plane home I sat next to a man who had written a book on spiritual healing, a seer who was a vegetarian like myself. He said I must take care of my body and stay healthy because I would eventually use a lot of physical energy in the spiritual work I would be doing. He instructed me to have energy work done on my body to aid me in becoming healthy. It was not enough to abstain from eating meat; I also had to make healthy choices in what I ate. I was also to find a teacher and learn how to become a channeler, he said. I was certain he had been put beside me to convey those messages, and I promised him and myself that I would do the work needed to keep me on my spiritual path. Meeting this man was an important piece in the puzzle unfolding in my life. I wanted more, but I had to learn that you are only given what you can handle at the time.

My life was changing in leaps and bounds. I was listening to my guides and following their direction. I attended lectures to hear more about spirits and psychic abilities. My guides told me that I had to learn everything I could in order to develop my gift, but at this point I didn't know what my gift was. They told me

I would be teaching others one day, and I had to work hard at learning my craft.

I was sitting in the audience at the New Life Expo in Manhattan and concentrating on the lecture when the woman on the podium said, "Spirits don't appear and stand in front of you. Manifestation is a thing of the past. What happens is that you hear a voice like your own intuitive voice in your head." She went on to say, "The spirits speak to me in voices, images, sounds, sensations, smells, tastes and feelings." When she was finished, the audience swarmed toward her.

I was excited because I received impressions the same way, and I knew I should study with this speaker. I could still hear the passion in her voice as she told the rapt listeners, "Learn to trust that voice in your head." However, the crowd around her was so dense that I couldn't get through, so I stood on the outside, looking in at what I wanted so badly. I wondered how I could tell Lucas that I had failed to make contact with the speaker since he'd been the one who had pushed me into going to the psychic expo to find a teacher.

I noticed a woman sitting on a table that had been shoved against the wall. I approached her and asked, "Does the woman who just spoke teach psychic development classes?" She cheerfully answered, "Yes. Out on Long Island." My face fell. Long Island was a long commute for an evening class. Then she said, "But I'm her teacher, and I teach in Manhattan." The weight of the world lifted from my shoulders, and in a flash I had enlisted Suzane Northrup as my first teacher. I didn't know that she was a well-known medium who would one day write the book *Seance: A Guide for the Living* which became one of the top books on mediumship in the late 1990s. I met with Suzane twice a month and began developing my gifts. I learned how to do psychometry which requires holding another person's personal object to get a message about that person. I sat in the dark to develop the ability to hear and see things. I had to learn all about the chakras, the centers of energy in the body. Meditation was an extremely important factor in my progress as it became the portal through which I meet my spirit guides and angels. There are meditation exercises to open and unlock the chakras and to keep the psychic work from turning into physical problems that would hinder my psychic abilities.

I had to learn discipline which was never easy for me. I had to do the work every day and not take little vacations from it. I had to look at people's strengths instead of their weaknesses and get rid of ego. I had to learn to depend on my guides and my teachers. I loved my studies and couldn't get enough.

I joined The First Universal Spiritualist Church and eventually did readings following the worship service. I love animals and early on was delighted to get a message from a little dog that had passed away. I was able to tell a woman that her dog had not been ready to leave earlier and was pleased that she had waited until she did to put him to sleep. The young woman had been guilt-ridden because she thought she had waited too long to have her dog euthanized. She had not told me about the dog before I spoke to her, so I knew that the message was correct.

I would feel wonderful after giving the messages and learning they were accurate, but later when I was alone, I would wonder if hearing these voices meant I was schizophrenic. I reasoned that people get locked in mental institutions for doing what I was learning to do, and I worried that I might be paying money to be crazy. The thought would pass, and I would know deep down that the work was something positive and loving. I knew something right was happening in my life, but I didn't realize that I was turning into a medium.

I considered myself a psychic because I received messages and passed them on to people. I did not want to be a medium. Psychics get messages from their spirit guides, and mediums talk to the deceased. The thought of talking to dead people was depressing and a total turn-off to me. I wanted to channel angels for people and make everyone happy and thereby save the world. I was a psychic. I was telling a fellow student that I thought mediumship was depressing when Suzane overheard me. She admonished me to not let the spirits hear me say that. There is a need and much healing from those who have passed, she said.

My job as makeup artist at Macy's brought me into contact with many people. I found that when someone spoke about a deceased loved one, I would feel the presence of the spirit. I got amazingly accurate information about the person. One day while working on a woman named Anna, I could see in my mind's eye that someone was standing beside her. She was a strong-willed, feisty woman accustomed to speaking her mind even more clearly than others wanted to hear. I had a feeling about the woman, but I wanted to be tactful, so I asked Anna, "Where is your mother?" There was sorrow in her voice as she answered, "She just died."

Her mother had been bedridden, and taking care of her had been Anna's life. Now she felt not only alone but also wished she could have told her mother that she loved her. I tried to be gentle as I told her, "I don't want to freak you out, but your mother is standing here," and I went on to describe her. Anna was delighted to hear that her mother was back to being her old self. The pain of her disease had buried her mother's feisty personality, and Anna had missed the person she had once been. Anna began coming to me for readings.

Word spread about my readings, and a young woman who worked at another cosmetic counter approached me. She was sad about the recent loss of her father whose sudden death came while he was in his forties. She did not understand how I could talk to a dead person and was apprehensive, to say the least. But she still wanted to try to talk to him. We went to the employees' lounge and contacted her father. I kept hearing the word "kitten" during the session. I asked if that meant anything to her. She told me that was his pet name for her. Kristen told her father how sad she was because he had to leave her, and he reassured her that he was well. He told her not to worry, that she would have a baby. She told me that she and her husband had been trying to have a baby for months, and she was starting to worry. Kristen felt better that she had her second chance to say goodbye, and she became pregnant within the year.

Kristen told everyone how pleased she was with the reading. She said that if the other employees had their way, I would be doing more free readings in the lounge than makeup in the cosmetics department. I did quite a few during breaks and at lunch time. Someone asked why I didn't charge for my readings if I was so good at them. I felt I couldn't charge because it was my gift, but I soon realized that I would not be respected if people did not pay. I began to hold sessions in my home, charging small amounts.

I started to attract groups of people to my home to have readings done. The spirit of my brother, Neil, would usually be present at the readings to act as my control. A control is a guide who sorts out which spirits will speak to the medium. This spirit decides who will approach the medium as well as how close they can come.

Neil also gave me confidence and kept me from being afraid. One evening when I started a session, I realized that my brother was not present. It was time for his soul to move on; he had other work to do. I now felt we had the relationship that never had a chance to grow in life which had been cut so short for him.

With Neil gone, I closed my eyes, meditated and opened the energy paths of my chakras. A Native American spirit appeared, and I soon realized that he was my control. The spirit stood straight and proud and told me his name, Great White Spirit. With him was a partner named Wind Chime.

As I did in every session, I started with a prayer, asking to give the person I spoke to what was needed to help on the path in this life. I asked that no spirit enter the room without permission from Jesus, the Christ. Great White Spirit was very organized and put a circle of sage around me, and the session began. When Great White Spirit started working with me, I realized that since I had a control, I was doing the work of a medium. My feelings were mixed. I was fearful because this was heavy work, and I didn't know if I was up to its demands. However, I wanted to help people. It was a lot for me to handle, and I was still unsure.

One night, Great White Spirit put a circle of sage around me, and the session began. The woman in the room started to cry, tears streaming down her face. She said, "I came here because my child is dead."

I could scarcely bear to look at her. If I talked to her child, it would make me a medium, but something was making me continue in spite of myself. "There are a lot of spirits here," I said weakly. Then I saw a bald, seven year-old boy lagging behind the other entities. I described the boy, and she told me that her seven-year-old son had died of leukemia. Then she started to cry harder. I told the boy that his mommy wanted to talk to him. It was very important to her. I asked him if he would come forward.

"I can't," he told me. "Every time I talk to Mommy, she cries. We used to be together all the time. Then I made her sad by becoming sick. I don't know why she's still sad. She wanted me to get well, and now I am."

When I told his mother what the boy said, she was startled at first but then wiped away the tears on her cheeks. She smiled as she hugged me and said, "Thank you. Oh, thank you! I will never cry again. Now I can say goodbye and let him be at peace." That was the last I saw of her, but I will never forget her and the little boy who had leukemia. Because of them, I knew that my calling was not to be just a psychic, but to be a medium. They helped me acknowledge my calling. I knew I could communicate with people who had died, and I knew I could bring comfort to those who loved them. I knew then that I was a medium, and I was grateful.

Part Two

Second Chances

The sun sets and the moon sets,
but they are not gone.
Death is a coming together.

--Rumi

CHAPTER 2

"If I Had Only Said Goodbye"

The death of a loved one is hard no matter how it happens. Whether you sit by the bedside and watch him cross over or feel the terror when your loved one is suddenly taken away, you will grieve. There is no easy way to go through this time without pain. We are never ready when that final moment comes.

With the help of my clients, their spirits from the other side and my guides and angels, I have put together the case studies in the next chapters. These case studies will help you understand how the spirit goes into transformation when different situations occur to cause the death of the physical body.

When we understand what the soul of our loved one is doing, it helps us feel like we have some control. Losing control is devastating to most human beings.

When I work with clients who are in the process of losing someone they love, I teach them how to discover what they actually can control, such as their ability to let go. Then when the death occurs, there grief is less. I also teach my clients how to go with the flow of life and accept whatever happens. They can then take an active part in helping their loved one to be unafraid and to stay in the moment of physical life until the body cannot house the soul anymore. By doing this, my clients understand that they have some sort of control. Without this understanding, you feel as if you're in a battle with death, a tug of war that you will eventually lose, and your loved one will be gone.

I received a call from my friend Eileen that her client Pat was dying. Eileen is a Reiki master and was helping ease Pat's pain. When I arrived, Pat was lying in his bed with labored breathing. Pat's wife, Marilyn, had made him as comfortable as possible. She moved a hospital bed into his favorite room in their house. There he lay with no pain medication as it was obvious he was in no pain, but Marilyn's heart was breaking because watching him lie there and deteriorate day after day was the most painful thing she had ever experienced.

I closed my eyes and opened up to the spirit realm. When I opened my eyes, I saw a spirit of a woman who told me she was Pat's mother. She was standing in the right corner of the room waiting for him. A younger man was behind her, but it was his mother whom Pat needed to accompany. I could feel resistance from Pat. I thought it was just because he was afraid to die.

When I told Marilyn what I was seeing, she told me that Pat's father died when he was two. She figured Pat would be very happy to go with him, but his mother had been very mean to him, and Marilyn didn't think he would want to go with her. Marilyn asked me why his mother was there for him now after the horrible things she had done to him when he was a child.

She told me she was sorry for being so hateful towards him. Before her soul could progress, she needed to make peace with her son. She also said, "We need to rid our souls of hate and anger. I am the one who has come to take him into the light."

I realized Pat was hanging on because he didn't want to go with his mother. I asked if he could go with his father. His mother told me, "No, he must come with me, and then his father will join us. We must make peace first."

I explained this to Marilyn and told her she had to help Pat make peace with his mother. I couldn't talk to Pat because he didn't know my voice. It was now up to Marilyn. Her heart was filled with sadness at the thought of letting her husband go, but she knew he couldn't go on this way. She agreed.

The next day I received a phone call. Pat had died that night. Marilyn told me that when she was given the job of helping her husband go to the light, it made his passing easier for her. She also told me she disliked his mother so much that it was very hard for her to help

Pat go with her. But as she sat with him that night, they all found peace.

I was called to the bedside of Anna Mae by her daughter Phyllis. Phyllis had taken her mother home when she realized her chances for survival were slim. Anna Mae was in her small room with all her wonderful belongings around her. As I watched her, I realized she was fighting very hard not to die, yet the cancer had taken over her body. She was barely conscious but knew I was in the room.

Phyllis sat with me, hoping Anna Mae would let go and move into the light. For months her mother had been lingering, slipping in and out of consciousness. Watching her mother, who once had a strong personality and was full of life, helplessly lie on the bed week after week was very hard for Phyllis.

Phyllis introduced me to Anna Mae. She understood that I was there and gave me a nod. I closed my eyes and began my meditation. I felt the spirit of Anna Mae's husband. He was standing by the big chair. He showed me his foot with a slipper on it. Phyllis told me her father had only one leg and often wore a slipper.

I took Anna Mae's hand and told her, "Your husband is waiting for you. It's okay to go with him." She nodded and tried to get out of bed and move to the chair.

At that point we knew she could see him. I told Phyllis that her mother was ready to let go. "She wants to go with her husband into the light, but she doesn't know how to go to him without taking her body with her. I explained to Phyllis how to help Anna Mae learn to move forward without her body.

For the next few days, Phyllis sat by her mother's side. She verbally and telepathically sent messages to her, asking her to let go of the control and float out of her body. She needed to leave her body behind, Phyllis gently repeated, because it was too sick to go with her. Within days, Anna Mae joined her beloved husband and moved into the light. Later Phyllis explained that taking the responsibility of helping her mother understand how to move to the light helped her with her grief. This task helped her forget her sadness when she realized there was a need for her help.

The death of a loved one is never easy. But if you know how to help them move smoothly into their final transformation, your focus turns to them rather than to your sadness. You now have a purpose in helping them cross to the light. From that point on, the bond between you will grow even stronger.

I watched my father lose his battle. He was ill for fifteen years, and the last few years were the worst. He had several heart attacks, but it was the Parkinson's disease that cruelly tore him down. I watched a man who was strong and a man I looked up to become frail and weak. His voice quivered as he forced sentences from his mouth. I watched my mother's fight to keep him alive.

My father had another heart attack and was very weak. After the heart attack he told my mother that when it struck, he felt himself floating away. After catching a glimpse of my mother's face in his mind, he came back. We thought he would live a little longer, so I went back to New York.

I was at work one Saturday afternoon when I received a telephone call. I was told to come home immediately as my father had taken a turn for the worse. The train ride was the longest two hours of my life as I faced the possibility of his impending death. He just couldn't die—not without my having the chance to say goodbye.

When I arrived, my father was screaming in agony as he was being prepped for emergency surgery. A hole had developed in the lining of his stomach and then had burst due to of all the medication he was taking. The doctors told us this operation would save him, so no one thought to say goodbye. When he returned from surgery, he wasn't my father. He was an unconscious, blown-up creature on a respirator with tubes protruding from him everywhere.

Dad was clinging to life because of my mother. My mother knew it was best to leave his side, to give him permission to die. Before leaving, my mother told him, "Go to the light. Go find Neil. It's okay."

At this time I had just returned to my spiritual path. I still had mixed emotions about letting him go. I was in awe of the strength my mother showed, but I wanted him to get well and live. I was not ready to say goodbye. I was not ready to let him die.

As soon as my mother left the room, my father started his transformation. I stared at the monitor and watched his heart grow weaker and weaker. Then I repeated my mother's words, "Go to the light."

I watched the monitor until it beeped for the last time. My father's lifeless body went on breathing because of the life support machine. I watched the nurse methodically turn off all the valves. I sat in a stupor. I could have said goodbye, but I had lost the opportunity because I was so focused on my emotional pain. He didn't have a chance to say anything to me, and I needed that so desperately. However, my mother had said her goodbyes. She felt as if she had some control in letting him go.

Afterward, my mother and I both longed for some reassurance that he was okay. We were hoping for a visitation or a dream, but we heard nothing. Two years after his passing, when I was well on my spiritual path, my father finally came to me and told me that he was all right.

Watching my father die, I realized that my whole concept of what it looks like to die was wrong. My understanding of dying was influenced by my mother's soap operas and the drama of the movies. Who could forget Melanie's death scene in *Gone With the Wind*? Long, drawn out goodbyes are often the norm in films, but in reality our reluctance to face the person's death prevents us from saying goodbye while they are still able to listen. By the time you accept the death, the person is often already in the process of his transformation and cannot respond to your words.

If the death was sudden, there was no time for goodbye. A client told me his eighteen-year-old son was on his way out the door and said, "Goodbye, Dad," but the father was so involved in his newspaper he did not respond. His son never came home. He died in an automobile accident that evening. My client felt that if he had only looked up from that paper and said goodbye, he would have had some sort of closure.

In reality, saying goodbye never feels right. Following are instances in which my clients had their second chance to say goodbye.

CHAPTER 3

Terminal Illness

When I left New York City and moved to Pennsylvania, my work changed. I was not able to see my clients in person anymore. Most of my business came from New York, and it was too far for my clients to drive to see me for a session. I began doing sessions over the phone, and to my surprise this method was easier and clearer. This opened a new world for me. People started calling me from all over the country for readings.

During my time of settling in Pennsylvania, I rescued a horse from slaughter. I was having behavior problems with this horse named Sioux, so I decided to call animal communicator Anita Curtis. Anita was fascinated with the work I did, and we decided to trade services.

Anita was going through a very hard time with the illness of her husband, Vic. He had been in the hospital for tests and suffered an allergic reaction to the dye that was put into his veins. His liver and kidneys shut down. Vic's lungs filled with fluid, and the blood tests for liver function were dangerously high. Even though he was not expected to live through the night, he managed to stay alive. He remained in critical condition for several days.

Anita sat by his bedside. She used her skills as a Reiki master to try to ease his transition to the other side. The doctors had said there was no hope of survival. After one Reiki treatment, Vic opened his eyes and looked at Anita and said, "They said I'm allowed to stay."

Anita asked, "Who are they?"

Vic said he had entered a large room and had been told to sit in a chair. Before he sat down, he saw a door and headed for it. He was told again to sit down. He looked around and saw a U-shaped table with twelve beings sitting around it. Their essence was of an orange color, and they were wearing shrouds. As Vic sat down in the chair, the beings leaned toward each other and spoke in low tones so Vic could not hear their words. One of the members of the council then turned to Vic and told him that he was going to stay on Earth. He opened his eyes and found himself in a hospital room with Anita by his side.

Vic was an atheist. His perception of death and of his own experience did not include the concept of heaven. He was comfortable with the scene he witnessed. This council was the beginning of his soul review in which it was decided that his time on Earth was not finished. He needed to go back.

Vic's liver tests improved the next day and were normal in a week. He lived for six years until he was diagnosed with cancer. Then his fight for life began once more. He was trained to be a survivor during World War II when he served as a Green Beret, and he had problems giving in to death. Anita nursed him at home. Each day seemed to be his last. Just as the life would be leaving his body and his soul was ready to take over, he would fight to stay alive a little longer. His lingering lasted for months.

Finally, Anita found the strength to say her goodbyes. She quietly talked to Vic and walked him through his final moment. When she left the room to get some rest, he let go of his physical body and finally passed on to the other side.

Anita waited to hear from him but heard nothing. Even though she said her goodbyes, she still wanted to know if he was okay. In her head she knew he had to leave his physical body, but her heart was filled with pain. She needed to spend a few more moments with him, so she called me.

I could see the grief in Anita's face when she came over for the session. I began to meditate and opened up my chakras, but I could not see Vic. My guide Great

White Spirit told me that Vic was not there. It was too soon. He had been taken straight up to the heavenly realm and was being nurtured in the healing chamber. He was moved from the Earth plane quickly because his connection with Earth had been so strong.

Weeks later, when I tried to reach him, I felt Vic's presence. He seemed very unsettled. He told me that he felt as if he lost the battle, and he wanted to come home.

In a grumpy voice he told me to tell Anita, "I met the members of my council again and was allowed to walk through the door. They told me that I need to disconnect from the materialism of Earth; then I can communicate with you. This is hard for me because I never envisioned an afterlife. Every soul here is loving and free from all worries. This concept is new for me."

He was angry about dying, and several times when we spoke to him, he was quite gruff. Vic stayed in his grumpy mood for a few more months.

Several months later, we tried again. This time Vic appeared with a big smile on his face. He looked younger and full of strength. His voice resonated when he spoke to me.

"Anita, it is very hard to be away from you," he said, "but in order to heal, I needed time."

"Are you happy?" Anita asked.

"I am learning," Vic answered.

"Where are you?" Anita inquired.

Vic had entered the celestial world. "I am in a place of peace," he said.

"What is your belief now?" Anita questioned.

"There are no beliefs here. It's all about love," he explained. "It doesn't matter whether you worshiped a God or not as long as your heart is full of love."

Vic, as a newly arrived spirit, sensed an expansion of consciousness on a spiritual level. "I have to leave. I feel a strong pull to Earth. Once I am at total acceptance of this side, I will be able to pass through the dimensions."

"What can I do to help?" asked Anita.

"Work on your acceptance of your new life. Then we can begin a new relationship."

I heard Anita sigh with relief and then say, "I will work hard to make that happen." Then Vic was gone, and I slowly opened my eyes.

Anita started doing the exercises I prescribed for communication. Vic appeared to her in a meditation. He seemed to be behind a veil that looked like a waterfall. They reached out to each other but could not touch. Vic understood what Anita was saying to him, but she could not hear him. He could answer her questions by nodding or shaking his head. Eventually, the information came in more strongly as the meditation exercises improved her vibrational levels. She could even feel him around her when she was doing yard work.

Both Anita and Vic are working very hard on accepting their new lives. Together, their soul communication has begun.

* * *

When Mary Catherine, a woman in her late sixties, called me, I vaguely remembered her from previous readings. There was something different about her. She seemed very unsettled in a peculiar way. I sensed a physical shift.

Closing my eyes, I quickly went into my meditation. I could smell the faint odors of cigars and whiskey. The image was clear: It was a man with a ruddy complexion and gray hair.

"I am seeing an older man. I am feeling pain in my head. It also seems as if he is wearing a pajama top with his pants." I asked her, "Do you know this man?"

She immediately confirmed that it made sense. "That's my husband," she said softly.

Her husband came through with a burst of anger. "What do you want?"

"This seems like a fairly new death," I said.

"My husband, Patrick, just died a few months ago," Mary Catherine said.

Patrick was adamant about getting the conversation over as quickly as possible. He wanted to bring closure to the relationship. "Tell her to stop the guilt," he told me. "It's okay. I know she wanted me to die."

I paused for a moment with the reading. Patrick's tone changed, and he suddenly asked for forgiveness. He instructed me to say, "I'm sorry for all the years of pain I put you through, the whiskey and the women.

When I went to my soul review, I sat and felt the pain I caused. You probably had every right to your actions after my behavior toward you. I know I have much spiritual work ahead of me. I will finally be at peace when I make amends to you and start dealing with the others I have hurt. I have a long road to travel as I heal."

"He is also telling me he wants you to go on with your career," I told her.

Mary Catherine seemed surprised. "He hated my passion for the piano," she explained. Her voice cracked. "His words were so cruel. I vowed to be rid of him when the children were old enough. We lived separate lives although we still occupied the same home."

Mounting pressure was building in my head. "Again, I am feeling pain throughout my head," I told her. "Did your husband's death have anything to do with a wound to his head or his brain?"

She answered, "Yes, his lifestyle caught up with him. The years of drinking took a toll on his body. His blood pressure was out of control, and he had a massive stroke. My career with the piano was put on hold again. I found I was spending more time driving him to his doctor appointments, cooking special meals and doling out medicines than even thinking about music."

I added, "I am feeling he was alone when he died."

Mary Catherine sobbed. "I just couldn't take it anymore," she cried. "I nursed him through his illness for years. I couldn't handle it. I put him in a nursing home and left him there to die. I was even happy when I received the call to tell me he had passed away. I thought my life would be happy, but the house became so empty, and now I feel so guilty." She broke down with those words, and I listened to her sob.

When she composed herself, I said, "Stop the guilt, stop the anger. Both of your souls met on Earth for special reasons. Learn from the lessons that the relationship gave to you and grow."

As the reading drew to a close, it was important to emphasize the issue with which most people have great difficulty: letting go. "The separation has finally come," I said. "Now you can both move on."

Patrick had a big smile on his face. "Patrick was telling me something about a waltz. He keeps repeating, 'Tell her about the waltz.'"

With a nervous laugh of embarrassment, she replied, "I play 'The Merry Widow Waltz' on the piano all the time."

* * *

I met Alice when I was seeing clients in New York City. She was young and overweight. Alice missed her mother so much that she thought she would try a reading, but she had no idea what to expect.

During my meditation I heard the word "father." I felt pains in my chest. "It seems to be his heart," I said. "Is that how your father died?"

"Yes," she answered. "His name was Edward."

Edward told me to tell Alice, "I had a very young mind, and I was trapped in an old body. I was very happy to go when I did. My soul is young and healed now."

Alice answered with amazement, "That sounds exactly like my father."

The next spirit that came through was a woman who told me, "I am her mother."

This time the pressure shifted to my lungs. It was hard to breathe, and my senses were filled with smoke.

Alice said, "Yes that's my mother. She had lung cancer. And yes, she did smoke."

With a worried look she cupped her mouth as if she was overcome with emotional trauma. She paused for a second and asked me, "Is she still smoking over there?"

I had to smile when I answered, "No, that's just her way of showing me that she is your mother. It's a way to recognize her."

"That's a relief," Alice said.

Her mother was eager to communicate. She spoke to me and said, "I didn't want to die. I fought very hard to stay alive. I was grateful for every extra day I had with you. I didn't want to be a burden, but I wanted to stay."

Alice answered, "That makes sense; it fits into the circumstances of her death. She died, was resuscitated and died for the final time. She fought so hard to stay alive. I felt guilty. I thought I was making her stay alive."

"She was worried about leaving you, and I am feeling there is a man whom she also worries about," I said.

Alice answered, "Yes, my brother."

Alice's mother went on to tell me, "At first, I didn't like being dead. I wanted to touch things. I missed my senses. Being in spirit was hard for me. After the healing chamber, as I started to lose my memories of the material world, things got easier. I felt comfort when I knew I could check on you any time. When your father joined me, my soul was complete. Alice, please take care of yourself. Watch your diet. Your food will eventually affect your health."

Before I closed the reading session, a woman in a wheelchair showed herself to me. "I just came to send my love to Alice," she said.

I described her and asked Alice if she knew this person.

She answered, "Yes, that is my cousin."

Months later, I heard from Alice, and she told me of the agonizing pain and torture her mother had to go through for many weeks. She said, "I began to see the situation differently after the session. I realized that it had been valuable time we had all spent together; valuable time we needed to spend together in order to survive without her. I also became a vegetarian and lost a lot of weight. I feel great. Thank you so much. This has given me great comfort. I've also come to look at many things in life differently now. I had always believed that I would be reunited with my loved ones some day. Now I have absolutely no doubt that I don't have to wait to be with them again. They are here with me right now."

***

Mary, a middle-aged woman from a deeply religious background, told me that she was apprehensive about having a reading. However, she needed answers to some questions concerning her sister's passing.

I assured her that I work from a place of God. She relaxed a bit, and we started the session. I closed my eyes and went into my meditation.

I saw a frail woman step forward. There was an inner strength about her in spite of her frailty, and she was quite serene. I felt burning pains in my right breast, and my body ached. I described what I was feeling and asked, "Does that make sense to you?"

Mary burst into tears. "Yes, that's Edna, my sister. She died of breast cancer."

I continued, "She is showing me that her right arm is in a sling. There is something unusual about the sling. It has a strange base to it."

Mary replied, "Yes, the lymph glands under her right arm were removed. After the surgery she lost most of the mobility of that arm and had to use a special sling with a wooden base."

The woman's spirit was eager to talk. "Tell my sister I saw Mary. My wish came true." Edna was showing me how the Virgin Mary helped her pass into spirit. A warm, glowing light surrounded her, and she held out her hand. Edna took her hand and rose from the bed. I told Mary what I saw and described the loving angels who surrounded Edna as they took her into the light.

"Now she's telling me that even though she was in so much pain, she did not want to leave. She was also worrying about a boy."

Mary said, "That is her son. She always worried about leaving her son."

Edna interrupted softly to say, "When I saw the Virgin Mary, I knew it was my time to go. Thank my sister for lighting the white candles."

Mary gasped, "I light white candles for her all the time."

I answered, "Edna feels the light of the candles and is aware of the love you send. She is getting ready to leave. Do you have any other questions for her?"

Mary said, "No. You have already answered the question that was on my mind. I was told by the woman who shared Edna's hospital room that Edna called out my name just before she died. Her roommate told me that even though there was a curtain around Edna's bed, she could see a glowing of light. She heard Edna yell out the words, 'I knew you would come, Mary.' Then Edna's beeper sounded, and the nurses rushed in. Her roommate told me that she was comforted to know that I was with Edna at the moment of her death. Surprised, I explained that I was not there. Deep in my heart I always wondered if the Virgin Mary came to my sister that night as she had always hoped and prayed. Now I know!"

CHAPTER 4

Abrupt Illness

I became acquainted with Erik and his mother while they were coming to me to complete their goodbyes to Erik's grandmother. At college Erik had met a girl named Christine with whom he wanted to have a romantic relationship. Christine insisted on keeping the relationship platonic because she was having a hard time dealing with the sudden death of her former boyfriend Brian. His death had stopped her twenty-two-year life. Erik knew she couldn't open up to another man until she was able to resolve what had happened. He knew how well he and his mother were doing with my help, so he urged her to call me. Christine was reluctant but so unhappy that she thought she would take the chance to talk to me.

I started with a prayer and meditation and went into a light trance. I saw a tall, young man holding a basketball. Christine said, "I believe that's Brian. We played basketball together all the time."

He told her, "I am in a wonderful place, and I am fine. I miss all my friends, but I come to visit."

She held back her tears as I continued, "Just know I'm okay, Chris, and it's okay to go on with your life."

"Did you know I was there?" she asked.

"He's telling me, 'Yes, Chris, I knew you were there.'"

Then I told her, "I feel as though I have a high fever."

She replied, "He had pneumonia."

"I also feel as if my body is very heavy, that I can't move."

She said, "Everyone had thought it was nothing, just a strong young man with pneumonia who would be out of the hospital in a couple of days. Someone came to me in class and told me to rush to the hospital. I was told that Brian's brain was bleeding."

"Brian was put on machines but became brain-dead. It was a terrible experience for me. I sat by his side and watched his condition worsen. It all happened so fast that it never occurred to me that I needed to say goodbye. The last time I saw him, he seemed to be getting better, but then he went into a coma and was dead in two weeks."

Brian told me, "I was very aware of everything and everyone around me. At times I floated above my body, looking down on my loved ones at my bedside. Then I started feeling a pull from the other side. I saw familiar faces of family members who had passed on, many of whom I knew only through photographs. They told me it was time for me to go. Once I decided to go to the other side, I felt the gravitational pull release. I could see a glimmer of light in the corner of the room near the ceiling. The light expanded and lengthened until it formed a large, tunnel-like pipe. The light looked soothing, and I did not try to resist as I floated toward it and into the mist." Brian continued, "The only word to describe my feeling was 'euphoric'. I began traveling through the white light on my journey to heaven."

Christine listened and then confessed, "I feel guilty about being the same age and alive. I feel guilty about wanting to be happy."

"He is telling me, 'It isn't a crime to go on living. I am happy where I am, and you can be happy where you are.'"

Before the session was over, I saw him holding a black-and-white cat. Christine looked surprised. "I had forgotten about that cat. It died a year before Brian." This made her confident that it was indeed Brian coming through, and she was happy that he and his cat were together again.

After they had said their goodbyes, Christine was able to start enjoying her life and began a healthy relationship with Erik. I was invited to their wedding and was delighted to be a part of the beginning of their new life together.

* * *

Carla was afraid that she would never be able to accept the death of her mother, Millie, but she vacillated between believing that someone who was a medium could help her and thinking that this psychic stuff was all rubbish. Eventually, Carla wanted to talk to her mother so much that she put her uncertainties aside and called me.

Carla said, "I have no questions to ask, but I want you to tell me anything you can. I'm a bit scared and nervous, but also excited about the reading."

As I opened my meditation, I felt the spirit of a woman come to me at once. She was easy to reach because she knew her daughter needed help.

I said, "There are two spirits with her, a female spirit and a weaker male spirit. The male spirit does not wish to talk but is obviously the female spirit's partner."

Carla confirmed, "Yes. They were Millie's mother and stepfather. Millie had never accepted having a stepfather and had nothing to do with him after her mother died."

Millie became impatient with all the discussion of family history and interrupted our conversation with, "Does my hair look nice?"

Carla laughed and said, "My mother would never miss her weekly appointment with her hairdresser because she felt so good when her hair looked right. Her hair was always perfectly cut and done in the latest attractive style."

At this time Millie became more serious and said, "You believe you didn't do enough for me, but I am so thankful for the way you took care of me. You knew how afraid I was of death, and you thought I would be terrified at the end, but I had help."

Millie went on to tell me that her mother appeared to her and told her what was going to happen and that she would be okay. All the fear left her, and she was at peace.

Carla started to cry uncontrollably.

I gently told Carla that Millie was saying, "I know I seemed out of touch with reality and cried about having to pay for my sins. I thank you for bringing the minister to me even though you thought I was out of my mind. The minister helped, but it was my mother who calmed me the most."

We had to stop the reading for a while until Carla stopped sobbing. As Carla wept, Millie said to me, "Please tell Carla not to feel guilty. I want to thank her for all that she did for me. I was so sick that I couldn't tell her, but I felt her presence and the love she had for me."

Carla composed herself and said, "I promised my mother I would take care of her when it was her time to die and that she would not have to be in a hospital. Her doctor did not believe she had become so sick so quickly. He insisted that she come to his office to be checked.

"I couldn't get my mother out of the car so the doctor came to the car to see her. He told me to take Mom to the hospital immediately. I wanted to take her home, but the doctor said I could not control her pain at home. As I drove to the hospital, Mom turned to me and said in a weak voice, 'Please don't take me to the hospital.' I tearfully told her that she would only be in the hospital for a few days, believing that she had months to live. I had stayed in the room with her overnight but could do nothing but watch my mother fade away. Mom died three days later."

I said, "Millie wants you to know that she had nursed her own mother during her final illness, and now you were doing the same for her."

Carla felt relief as she said, "I'm glad she knows how much I did for her and how much I loved her."

Millie is telling me, "My mother was at the bedside as I died and brought me through the tunnel of light to the other side. I could feel both the warmth of the light and the love of my mother as we went together to the heavenly realm."

As we were completing the session, I said, "I'm not sure if Millie is saying that there is a message about your son or about your son-in-law."

Carla said, "I have no son." I asked if one of her daughters was married. Carla said, "One of them is engaged, but none are married."

I heard Millie chuckle and say, "You'll see."

Several weeks went by, and Carla called to tell me that her daughter had been married secretly before our call, and she did indeed have a son-in-law. I asked how Millie had been at keeping secrets. Carla was delighted to tell me that Millie had never been able to keep from telling what she knew. It was fun to hear about the secret marriage, but it was wonderful to hear the serenity in Carla's voice as she spoke of her mother. The goodbyes had been said, and Carla and Millie were both at peace.

CHAPTER 5

Sudden Death

There are no goodbyes when someone you love is taken away from you suddenly. Within minutes your world changes, and you are not prepared for the shock.

The news usually comes from a phone call or a knock at the door. This scene plays through your head repeatedly. The anticipation of reliving those moments becomes unbearable. For years after my brother's death, my mother felt a sick feeling penetrate her stomach every time she heard the phone ring.

Sudden death leaves many unanswered questions. My clients usually want to know if their loved ones suffered and if they are at peace now. The chance to say goodbye is very important as a sense of closure. It allows the grief process to begin and bring healing.

When I started my meditation for Alan's reading, I went into a light trance. I felt a terrible pain in my chest. I knew I was about to hear from someone who had experienced a major heart attack.

"I am feeling the presence of a man in his fifties. I feel a heart attack."

My client Ruth knew at once that this was her husband. "That is Alan. He was fifty-four."

I asked, "Did he play golf? He is showing me golf clubs. He is also saying the word 'anniversary.'"

Ruth started to cry and said, "Oh my God, that's Alan. He had a massive heart attack while we were playing golf. It was our twenty-fifth anniversary."

I felt Alan's spirit come through. He said, "Tell Ruth that I was there trying to comfort her as she knelt beside me. I tried to hug her, but I couldn't. I saw a brilliant light and saw my father within the light."

As Alan continued, I told Ruth, "Alan is telling me that he hardly recognized his father. Does that make sense to you?"

"Yes," Ruth responded. "His father died when Alan was very young."

I continued to put into words Alan's messages: "I was so happy to see my father. I felt myself disconnected from the pull of Earth. It was as if all of my emotional attachments faded away. I was delighted to be going on the journey with my father."

Ruth's curiosity got the better of her, and she asked, "Did you feel dead?"

Alan hesitated briefly and then told me to explain, "Death is only a matter of consciousness. I feel very much alive. You will find yourself in whatever circumstance you believe. If you think death is confinement in a box in the ground, that is where you will be until you believe otherwise."

Ruth was confused. "How will you get to believe otherwise?"

I heard Alan's patient reply, "Your guides will teach you how to move on."

I felt a sadness come over Alan as he said, "I am so sorry that I hadn't put all of my affairs in order. The legalities have caused you so many problems."

Ruth nodded when I told her what Alan had said and answered, "It's fine now. I managed."

I saw a loving smile on Alan's face and heard the word "friend." I told Ruth, "Alan is trying to tell me something about his friend."

Ruth looked shocked. "What about his friend?"

Alan smiled and said, "Tell Ruth that my friend is okay. I sent him to her."

I asked Ruth if she understood what I was telling her. "Alan is very persistent about letting you know about his friend."

"Alan is a very persistent man." She looked away from me and said, "I'm dating his friend. I feel so guilty about it, but I feel close to Alan when I'm with his friend."

Alan was adamant about being heard. He said, "Tell her it's all right. I sent my friend to her because I couldn't stand seeing her so lonely. Tell her, 'I watched you wish for death to take you. I will always love you, but I cannot fulfill your physical needs. My friend can do that for the rest of your time on Earth. Remember, even through death, nothing can separate our souls. Just be happy.'"

Ruth sounded relieved when she asked, "Are you happy?"

Alan told me, "Yes. My transition was easy. I felt the embrace of love. I did not suffer on Earth for any length of time, so I did not have to spend too much time being healed. I was soon able to join my group soul."

I told Ruth that Alan was now leaving. They both said their goodbyes with love. Ruth told me that she felt a sense of closure and relief. She felt that she could now find happiness.

* * *

Bob and Tina were so comfortable together that I just knew they had been with each other through many lifetimes. Bob told me that he didn't know what was supposed to happen during a session, but he came to make Tina happy. After Bob explained his skepticism to me, he settled into an easy chair and sat quietly.

Tina asked to speak to her spirit guides. I told her that I don't call any spirits in particular. I just open up and pray for whoever needs to be here. Tina was a bit disappointed but was willing to see what would happen.

I closed my eyes, began my prayer and went into a light meditation. I suddenly smelled cigarettes and could barely see through the thick smoke. I felt the presence of spirits in the room. When I could finally see through the haze, I saw the silhouettes of two elderly women having a heated argument. I could tell these two souls were stuck in old patterns.

I looked at Tina and asked, "Are your mother and grandmother on the other side?"

Tina nodded and replied, "Yes. They are both there."

I said, "I feel the air is very thick with cigarette smoke. The two women are arguing. Does that make sense to you?"

Tina said, "They are my mother and my grandmother. They always argued, and they smoked like chimneys."

Tina did not seem to be happy with these spirits, so I searched hard to see someone else. Bob cleared his voice and asked if he could try to reach someone. He handed me some military medals and said he hoped I could contact a spirit through them.

The spirit of a man in his early forties was there immediately. I knew at once that he had a quick death. I told Bob about the man, and he sighed and said, "Yes, that's him. That's my father, Martin. He died in an automobile accident when he was in his early forties. You're exactly right."

"Martin is telling me that he is sorry you were bitter about his death. He knows it was hard for you."

Bob agreed.

Martin told me to let Bob know that he has work to do on the other side. I told Bob, "Martin is a greeter of spirits. He helps them get used to their new surroundings. He says that when someone dies early in life, there is usually work for them in this realm. He is very good at his work and quite proud of it."

Bob smiled, but then the tone of Martin's message changed. I said, "Now Martin is showing me that he is worried about someone. I am hearing the word 'mother.' The man she is married to is abusive. He says not to take any action. The abuse will stop soon. There is karma between the two of them that must be completed. Do you understand that?"

Tina spoke up, "I told Bob recently that I was worried about his mother's bruises and some broken bones. I was beginning to suspect that the stories about being clumsy were not true and that her husband was hurting her."

Bob added, "My brother is also suspicious."

Martin changed the subject once more. I told Bob, "I am hearing Vietnam. Were you there?"

Bob said he was.

"Martin is telling me that he is very proud of you. He wants you to know that you can reach him on your own any time you need to."

The spirit of Martin disappeared as quickly as it arrived, and the session was over. Bob now felt a connection with his father. There was a new sense of hope in his relationship with his father on the other side.

I heard later from Bob that his mother's husband started having epileptic seizures a few days after the reading and was too weak to be a threat to his mother. He was still verbally abusive to her, but she was so used to his outbursts that it did not bother her. However, Bob's mother became fully responsible for her husband's care, continuing to work on the karmic relationship they agreed upon before coming into this life.

Within a few months Bob did start a new relationship with his father's spirit. He is no longer a skeptic.

* * *

When I spoke to Carol, she seemed at first to be very composed as she tried to hold herself together for the session.

I started Carol's session with my prayer and light trance. "I see a woman with curly hair," I told her. "She is coming to me first. Another woman with a very stern look on her face is standing off to the side. They are showing me that they did not get along in life. Do you recognize these women?"

Carol identified them, "They are my mother and my grandmother. They never had a good relationship."

I continued to hold a dialogue with Carol based on thoughts and impressions I received from her grandmother. Then I said, "I feel tightness in my chest and am having trouble breathing. There is also a difficulty walking because of a problem with my foot."

"Yes," Carol replied. "That's my mother."

I went deeper into a trance. "I see a beautiful young girl. She has sandy brown hair. Her energy is vivacious. Wait. Now I feel BOOM! My head hurts." I instinctively grabbed my head in my hands. "Another sensation is coming into my mind. I feel like I am running. I want to keep running, but I know I am flying. There is no more pain. I feel wonderful.

"Now I'm looking down and see a body sprawled on the pavement. The young woman is telling me, 'I saw my body lying there, but I never went back to it. I didn't feel anything, but there was a lot of confusion and chaos going on.' Do you know what I am talking about?" I asked.

Carol's voice was filled with emotion, "Yes, that's my daughter Kelley. She was chasing someone. That was part of her job as a correctional officer. The loud boom was part of her death. She was hit by a van last December as she ran into the street."

I said, "This is confusing. You said December, but she is wearing summer clothing."

"Oh yes, she would be wearing those clothes. She died in Arizona."

Kelley continued to tell me, "Grandma helped me through the confusion. She helped me go to the light."

Carol asked me to thank her mother and then asked Kelley, "Are you with Grandma?"

Kelley told me to tell her mother, "No. I have my own work to do."

Carol said she wasn't surprised. Then Carol's mother pulled my attention to her. She said, "You can tell Carol that my guides want me to heal, but they told me I could take as long as I want. I was sick for a long time. I have free will. I don't have to heal yet if I don't want to. I am just beginning to get over the memories of my illness. Nobody knows what I had to go through..."

Her rambling speech would have gone on, but Kelley made her presence known again by gently smiling. I could tell that her grandmother amused her. Kelley told me, "I lived my life very quickly. I felt like I was always a step ahead of where I was supposed to be going. I guess I always knew I wasn't going to be there long. I want to thank you for being my mother. You understood me and gave me freedom. We were friends."

Carol's "thank you" was filled with sadness. She perked up a little when she asked Kelley, "What do you think of my wellness center?"

"She's telling me, 'I was there when you created it.'"

"You were my inspiration," Carol responded.

Carol's mother drew my attention once again and said, "I inspired you, too. After all, you went through my unwellness to create wellness. That's a form of inspiration."

"She hasn't changed," Carol said with a laugh.

Carol was able to say goodbye to the old relationship she once knew. She put closure to the death that took her daughter away so suddenly. Carol is now helping others cope with their grief. She is teaching them to open their minds to other realms. Kelley is by her side, and both souls are growing together.

CHAPTER 6

Suicide

I have spoken to many souls who have committed suicide and have found a common thread running through their stories. Before we are born, we agree to a certain life and to be with certain people. We have free will, and if we decide to commit suicide instead of fulfilling that commitment, it is our choice. However, there will be consequences if we decide not to honor that which we have agreed to do.

We will have to watch our loved ones as they deal with our death. The family of a child who committed suicide will feel guilt and wonder if there was something they could have done to prevent it. The husband of the wife who killed herself will feel he should have listened more. Maybe then he would have heard her plea for help.

I had one client whose husband could not bear to think that he could not take care of his family. After he committed suicide, his spirit had to watch as his family lost everything and was forced to live in a shelter. He had given up the opportunity to care for them, and now his pain continued even on the other side. The anguish felt in an unhappy life does not just disappear or die. Even though the physical body and the brain die, the mind lives on. The memory of the suffering is still there, so you will still be aware of it when you get to the other side.

After healing and learning with others in the group soul, the spirit will begin to understand. The soul will determine why there was a blockage to happiness in its life on Earth.

The soul will stay in its group soul until it understands what went wrong in life. When the soul is truly ready, it will come back and try to learn its lessons again. Life on Earth will he harder this time. This is why the soul takes its time to reenter another physical body.

If one kills oneself to be with a loved one, there is no guarantee of togetherness in the afterlife. The lessons each soul will need to learn will be different, and they will be in different soul groups.

Being on Earth is a gift because one can learn many lessons here. The experiences here are endless. When we are in despair, we must wait. If we wait long enough, the darkness will slowly leave, and the light will shine through.

Renee had gone to other mediums for readings since this topic fascinated her. She had heard of me from a friend and was excited that I was in the same state. When she called for her session, as always, I began my meditation with a prayer. I closed my eyes and focused into the darkness.

The spirit of a young man came to me. I could tell he had a strong bond with her, and I noticed that he had a most unusual smile. His eyes narrowed, but his face seemed to light up with joy. He had dark hair and was quite good looking. I also felt a problem with his breathing. My breath became very labored.

I described him to Renee, and she said, "That is my brother, Steve. He suffered from asthma. He is the one I hoped to talk to."

Steve seemed anxious to get started with the reading. I felt that his death was very sudden. Renee hesitated and then said, "Yes. Go on."

"He is showing me a man that is with him. I am hearing the word 'grandfather.' I feel paternal. Was this grandfather in spirit when Steve arrived?"

Renee answered, "Yes, he was named after him. People in our family would say they shared the same personality."

"Steve is telling me his grandfather was there when he woke up. He is emphasizing the words 'woke up.' My body also feels drugged."

I understood when Renee explained, "Steve ended his life by taking an overdose of sleeping pills."

Steve wanted me to tell her that Grandpop was very disappointed in the way their father treated both him and Renee.

Renee acknowledged that their father was cold and self-centered whereas their grandfather had been known to be a compassionate man.

"Now I am feeling that there is a strong alcohol content in my body. Steve is telling me the alcohol gave him the courage to take pills."

Renee answered, "You're right. We were surprised when a bottle of alcohol was found near his body. He was not a drinker."

"He is also telling me about headaches and stomach pains."

Renee said, "I didn't know about that until I found a bottle of aspirin in his car." Then she hesitated, "Come to think of it, one of his friends told me Steve was concerned about an ulcer."

"Was Steve married?" I asked.

"Yes, why?"

"I believe Steve was having problems with his wife," I said softly to prepare her for the next information I was to tell her. "This situation might have pushed him to the suicide." I also asked, "Was he being accused of something?"

Renee explained, "Yes. I found out that Steve's wife had taken out a protection from abuse order. Steve always took pride in his honesty and integrity. He had a bad temper at times, but he was never violent. He had lived with his future wife for three years before marrying her.

"The relationship went downhill as soon as they were married. I was so shocked about the accusation that I called some of his old girlfriends. They confirmed that he never showed any signs of violence. I found out later that Steve's wife was having an affair. She married her lover shortly after Steve died."

As I focused my energy, I saw Steve's spirit with his head down. I described his posture to Renee and told her, "This situation really hurt him. But he is telling me he is at peace now. He knows he'll have to deal with his choice one day, but right now he is healing."

Renee said, "I am so happy that he is at peace."

"He is also telling me even though he was raised by an atheist, he had hoped that Jesus might come to him. It was a wonderful surprise when Steve saw him.

"Now Steve is showing me a watch and saying, 'Tell her about the watch.'"

Renee gasped. "I know what he means. Steve's gift to me one Christmas was a watch. I am wearing it on a chain around my neck right now. You couldn't have known that."

"Now he is saying something about swimming. 'Swim for relaxation.' Do you understand this?"

Renee laughed, "I love to swim to relax. It was a joke we shared because he was very athletic, but I could outswim him."

"Before Steve leaves, I see him handing you a brown wooden box. I hear the word 'photographs.' He also wants you to use the items in it. Do you know what that means?"

"No," Renee said in a puzzled voice.

"I feel this box has items in it that belonged to Steve."

"I have a suitcase with his things in it."

Doubting myself, I said, "It could be, but it really feels like a wooden box. Now it is time for him to leave. He must go back to his work on the other side."

When Steve had gone, Renee told me that she felt guilty because she saw him just before he died and did not realize that anything was wrong. She thought she should have felt his pain since he was not only her brother but also her friend. She realized that she missed the chance to say goodbye.

I received a Christmas card from Renee. She told me that the day after the reading, she remembered a brown wooden box that Steve gave her before he died. She had tucked it away. When she opened it, she found the photographs and a pen set. She thanked me for giving her the Christmas present of the wooden box.

* * *

When Pam called me to set up an appointment, I could hear the despair in her voice. She told me she wanted to talk to her son Jimmy, and she wanted him back.

I told her we would talk during our session. I hung up the phone and said a prayer for her.

On the night of our session, I could still feel the deep sense of sadness in Pam's voice. I did not know Jimmy's story but hoped he would help his mother heal.

As I opened from my meditation, I could hardly breathe. My throat was closing up, and I could feel the presence of a young man.

I asked gently, "Is Jimmy a teenager, and did he hang himself?"

My heart went out to Pam as I waited for her to compose herself enough to answer.

Finally I heard her say, "Yes, Jimmy was fifteen when he hung himself. I miss him so much and would give anything to have him back."

I explained to her that this was impossible. "Jimmy tells me he wasn't happy here. He is not ready to come back. He needs time. But once he heals, you can find the bond you once shared with him and build a new relationship." Pam listened to me, but I wasn't sure she believed this concept that was new to her.

I asked if he suffered from mood swings.

Pam answered sadly, "Yes, but he really had no reason to be depressed. Everyone loved him. Many people attended his funeral."

"He is telling me he is sorry, but he wanted to die. He felt living was hard. He did not feel a part of the Earth. He wanted to get out of life. He thought it would be easier on the other side, but it is not. Now he is telling me about a dog. I think he wants his dog. Does that make sense to you?"

As Pam cried, she told me that Jimmy's dog had become sick on Jimmy's birthday. "I am afraid the dog is going to die. I will understand if the dog is supposed to go with him. I even thought of euthanizing her, but that dog is my last connection to my son."

I told Pam that the longer the dog remains here, the sooner Jimmy's obsession with her will leave. He needs to learn to let go and learn more discipline. If Jimmy had always been stubborn, death would not change him immediately. It takes time to change. His angels and guides were working with him in order to heal his pain, but it seemed that Jimmy was making slow progress in that area. I told Pam about the group soul sessions in which Jimmy would have to participate in order to heal.

Then Jimmy confirmed to me that he had been working and growing spiritually with others who felt the same way as he did and who also committed suicide.

Pam started to cry, "I failed as a mother."

I heard Jimmy say, "No, Mom, you always showed me love. I argued with everyone. I just couldn't get it together."

Through her sobs Pam said, "We found him, but it was too late. The police ransacked his room searching for drugs but found nothing. I fixed his room the way it used to be. Sometimes I go into it and yell at him for leaving. Does he know that?"

I smiled as I told her Jimmy's reply, "Yes, I know."

"Now I am feeling pain in my chest, but it doesn't feel like a heart attack. I see two people coming through. They seem to be an older man and woman. Could these be Jimmy's grandparents?"

Pam replied, "Yes, my father passed with lung cancer, and my mother followed with breast cancer."

I told her, "They were with him to help him through his transformation."

Pam's mother asked me to thank Pam for caring for her before she died.

Pam acknowledged, "I did look after my mother."

Within minutes the spirits were gone, and the session was closed.

Jimmy will be able to learn with other souls. He will join with those who have taken their own lives and will finally have the feeling of belonging. He will have to live out the life he cut short when he returns to Earth, but he will be better able to cope because of the healing he is going through now.

It will take Pam a long time to say goodbye to the life she knew with Jimmy, but she can still have him in her heart and feel his love as she sits by herself in his room.

* * *

I consider this story to be quite unique in the realm of saying goodbye. The events all started to unfold when Diane called just to see who would communicate with her. She was going through a difficult time in her life and wanted to know if a guide or someone from the spirit world could help her.

When I opened from my prayer and meditation, I felt a spirit of a man. I knew this man had suffered for a long period of time. I did not feel that his was a new death. I sensed that he had been in spirit for a while as he was very settled. I felt the deep love he was sending to Diane. I told Diane what I was receiving.

Diane responded immediately, "It's Hal, I know it is." She thought a moment and then asked, "Now, does he know what I meant."

I told her Hal answered quickly, "Yes, I know what you meant." Diane laughed and then explained that when she told Hal that she believed in spirits, psychic phenomenon and even communication with animals, he had told her she was crazy.

Hal told me to tell Diane, "I am with you often."

Diane was very open to Hal's presence. During the reading she could feel him. I told her, "Just trust it."

They chatted about a business venture that Diane was starting, and then the reading was over.

A few months later, Diane told me that after her session with me, something had happened, and she was able to hear Hal's voice. One day while driving in her car, a song came on the radio that was their favorite song. When she heard the song, her mind went to Hal. She heard his voice in her head. He told her that he was very happy about her business venture, and she could feel his joy.

She thought about contacting me to share the experience but got too busy and let it pass. Weeks later, again in the car, the same song came on, and she heard Hal's voice tell her to get in touch with his son Peter because he was in trouble. Diane thought she was imagining his voice and changed the station. She had not seen Peter for some time and did not think there was anything wrong with him. Diane said she would have called me then, but she was still quite busy and just didn't get around to making an appointment.

The next week as she was driving, she heard the same song and got the same message from Hal. Diane tried to reach Hal's children as soon as she got home, but she could not get through to them. Hal was persistent. The song came on once more, and she heard the same message from her departed friend.

Diane was becoming quite disturbed but still did not take the time to have a session. One week later, she was in an out-of-the-way antique store in downtown New York when she heard someone call to her. She looked up and saw Hal's youngest son who lived in Connecticut. Diane was relieved to see the young man. She told him that she had a message from his father. He looked skeptical, but then he asked what the message was. She told him that Hal wanted her to get in touch with Peter because there was a problem.

He said, "There sure is a problem. Peter's back on dope."

Diane contacted Peter and told him his father was warning him to straighten out.

Diane called Peter as often as she could and tried to help him see where his current path was leading him. One day during a visit to Hal's grave, Peter cried and promised to straighten out, but soon afterward he relapsed. Peter did not return Diane's calls, and eventually, she lost touch with him. Two months later, Peter's brother called to tell Diane that Peter killed himself.

Diane was devastated and felt guilty. Her emotional state blocked her ability to hear messages from Hal, and she desperately wanted to speak to him, so she called me.

I had no idea what had happened since our last session. I recalled seeing Hal's spirit in a joyous mood when he saw Diane, but this time he had a somber look on his face. The tone of his voice was serious.

"I feel that there is a new death around this man, and Hal is telling me to tell you that it was not your fault. Do you understand that?" I asked.

"Yes, I understand," she replied. "His son Peter died."

I explained to Diane, "Hal wants you to know that Peter never got over his mother's death. She died when he was very young. Peter never felt like he belonged here after she died. Now Hal is showing me that he and Peter's mother met Peter after the suicide. He wants you to know he and Peter finally got the chance to make amends. They spent a lifetime hurting each other. Now they are healing."

Diane asked, "Is Peter there?"

I could see Hal shaking his head, "no." Hal said to let Diane know that Peter is in a place of healing. He has lessons to learn since he did not fulfill his contract in his life as Peter. Hal said, "I cannot help him now, but his mother can. They are together."

Later I realized that Hal and his son had a second chance to say goodbye from the other side, and the healing will continue for all of them.

CHAPTER 7

Murder

As we discussed in the previous chapters, accepting a death is difficult. When a person is trying to accept the death of a loved one who was murdered, the emotions are intensified in different ways. Because of the circumstances surrounding murder, there are often many unanswered questions.

One goes through the different stages of grief, and most of the time, the stage of anger is the most difficult to release. The hardest task a human might endure is to find forgiveness in her heart toward the person who committed the crime. We don't have the right to judge the circumstances of life, however. We must remember that we are all part of a divine plan. No matter what happened to your loved one, he is at a place of healing and peace now.

The question I am asked most frequently is, "Did he feel the pain?" Family members of the victim often recreate the scene of the crime over and over in their heads. You must let it go. The soul is usually thrown out of the body instantly, and the person feels no pain. It's the cases in which the body was tortured before the death that most people worry about. In my experience the angels of the victims take them out of the body before the act is completed. Even if they are still alive, their awareness is not there. The scene in the family's head is usually far worse than the actual experience of the soul.

Another prominent stage for those left behind is that of guilt. They feel they did something wrong, and the murder was somehow their fault.

For those who are caught in any of these stages after the murder of a loved one, I strongly urge you to first get help so you can move on. Then it would be a good idea to contact your loved one to get comfort. Know that the spirit of your loved one is now safe. Forgive yourself and then forgive the murderer.

I hope that by reading these case studies, you will be able to understand how the soul finds peace, so you can begin your road to healing.

* * *

A man named Nick came to my New York City apartment for an appointment. He showed up for the reading for a specific reason, and his tone was abrupt and angry. I took a deep breath, closed my eyes and asked my guide to help me. I knew this wasn't going to be easy.

I went into my meditation, and soon a young girl about fifteen was smiling at me. She had a beautiful smile with perfect teeth. Her hair was blond and hung neatly on her shoulders. She was also wearing a red jacket. I described this young girl to the man seated before me.

Nick's voice changed to sadness. "That is my daughter Amanda," he said. "She was fifteen, and her favorite jacket was red. As a matter of fact, she was wearing it the day she died."

I looked into his stern eyes. "I feel pressure in my throat. I feel as if I can't swallow. There is a lot of fear. Now I am feeling sharp pain in my pelvic area. Was she murdered?" I asked.

"Yes, she was sexually molested, then strangled."

"She wants you to know she is okay. She keeps repeating to me," I explained, "'Daddy, it's okay. You need to let it go. I am very happy where I am. Please stop reliving my death. But most of all, it was not your fault. Understand, Daddy, it was not your fault.'"

"Tell her it was my fault. It was!" he shouted.

"Now she is telling me about your work. She wants you to find your passion again."

His shouts turned into sobs. "No, it was because of my passion with my work that I lost her!"

"Your daughter is telling me that she wants to comfort you. She is saying to me, 'Tell Daddy it was just my time.'"

"I should have been there on time to pick her up," he explained. "She was waiting for me after school. I let her wait because I was so involved with my work. While she was waiting, she was dragged into an abandoned factory building and murdered. Mandy, I am so sorry I let you down," he cried.

"She is saying to me, 'No, you never let me down. You are disappointing me now. All the love you had has turned to hate.'"

Then I asked, "Are you trying to find her murderer?"

"Yes I am. I want him to suffer the way my daughter did," he said.

"She doesn't want you to do that. She is telling me, 'Daddy, let it go. Your hate is destroying your life. Stop reliving my murder. It is worse in your mind than it was for me.'"

He ignored his daughter's message and asked, "What happened?"

I felt myself being pulled into a scene. She was taking me to a huge, dirty room, and I was almost afraid to look at what she was showing me.

Then in my mind, she started to explain: "I walked a few blocks to find a pay phone to call you. I was so busy listening to my headset that I didn't realize two young men were following me. They grabbed me and pulled me into an abandoned building. They took turns holding me down by the neck and sexually molesting me. I was full of fear, but I kept fighting. It all happened quickly. Within seconds I felt no more pain. I must have passed out from the lack of oxygen. The man did not realize I had stopped fighting and was pressing very hard on my neck until it broke. I felt myself floating above the horrible scene. Before I had a chance to wonder what was going on, I heard a soft voice say, 'I am your angel.' I turned my head and saw a very beautiful woman. Her expression was sincere and loving. She told me she didn't want me to think she let me down. My death was supposed to happen this way. She said she took me out of my body as soon as she could so I would not suffer."

When I ended his daughter's message, Nick's voice was faint but still full of rage. "They must pay for what they did to you!" he said to his daughter.

She answered gently, and I repeated, "They will have to deal with what they did when they come to the other side."

He started sobbing and could barely choke out the words, "It's not enough!"

"Amanda is telling me that one is already in prison for another crime," I told Nick. "The other lives in the hell that he has made for himself. God has a way of making restitution. You don't have to take His role."

"If there were a God, he wouldn't have taken you away from me," he lashed out.

Amanda wanted me to repeat, "It was time for me to go. It was going to happen that day, and you were delayed so that my death could occur." She continued, "We can now say goodbye to the relationship we once knew, but our souls will always be connected. We have a bond that will never be broken. Please, Daddy, find your peace. I have found mine."

Then she was gone.

I could only hope the session helped this grieving and anger-ravaged father. Amanda gave him his chance to say goodbye.

* * *

I received a phone call from a woman named Debra. She was very soft-spoken. I asked her if there was anything she wanted me to focus on during the session. She told me "no" and seemed very vague. I didn't think much of it and closed my eyes and began my meditation. I went into a light trance and soon saw a woman standing in front of me. I described her to Debra, and she said it was her mother. This woman was also very quiet, and there was a feeling of sadness about her.

A man soon joined her. I felt terrible pains in my head, especially around my eye. I asked Debra, "Could this be your husband, and did he have a stroke?"

She answered, "Yes, it is my husband, Nino, but he did not have a stroke."

"He was telling me that his pain is gone," I continued, "but I was still getting the sensation of pain in my head and one eye."

Debra calmly replied, "That makes sense."

I was feeling a quick death and a force of being thrown out of the body. The pain was an impact to my head. Then I realized what the pain was from.

I asked, "Was he shot?"

She softly replied, "Yes."

"He is telling me that it took him a long time to accept what had happened to him. He was in shock at first. He wants you to know that he wanted to stay to help you."

"I'm sure," Debra replied. "Did he suffer?"

"He is explaining to me that he did not suffer. He was thrown from his body at once. The hardest thing was not the pain but watching the body die and being desperate to help you. He wasn't ready to go.

"Now he is saying the word 'mother.' I think he is referring to your mother. She was there at his death, and when he was overwhelmed with confusion about leaving you, she told him that she would show him the way."

"Is his father in spirit?" I asked.

Debra answered, "Yes."

"He is letting me know that his father also came to be with him. Now he is showing me both of them taking him into the light."

Debra listened.

"He is telling me that he wasn't permitted to see what was going to happen to you. There were times when he could come to you when you were alone on the bed. He wanted to tell you that you were going to hear some bad news, but that he was really okay. He tried, but you couldn't hear him."

I did not understand what was going on but hoped it made sense to Debra.

"Yes," she said, "when I was tied to the bed, I did hear him. I heard, 'hang in there, honey.' I didn't know if it was him or my mother."

"Now he is telling me something about his family. He seems disappointed."

Debra asked, "What about his family? What should I do? They won't speak to me."

He explained to Debra, through me, "He doesn't like the way they've been treating you, but he is even more upset by the way they ignore the children. He is especially disturbed at how they treat his son. He wants you to know that you don't deserve that treatment. You didn't do anything wrong."

Debra said, "We have a son and daughter. Our son has a chronic illness and is about to graduate from college. My husband's family ignores him, and they blame his father's death on me."

"He is telling me he loves you very much and to be happy with your new life. He wants you to know your souls will always be connected."

With that he was gone, and the session was over.

Debra thanked me and apologized for being so vague. She explained that her ordeal had been reported in the papers and on television, and she did not want me to know who she was. I cradled the phone on my shoulder and poured myself a cup of tea while she told me her story.

Debra Puglisi was in her rose garden in a quiet neighborhood in Delaware. A man who was stalking the neighborhood decided to kidnap her. He broke into her house and, without Debra hearing a thing from the garden, shot and killed her husband who had come home at the same time. The murderer went outside, grabbed Debra and forced her into his car. Once he had her in his home, he tied her to his bed and raped her repeatedly.

Days later, while her hands were tied to the bedpost, a blaring television report delivered the news of her kidnapping and showed the crime scene with her husband's body. She realized her husband was dead, and the pain was unbearable. Her nightmare had worsened. Then, when she felt she couldn't go on, she felt her husband's presence. That was when she felt him on the bed and heard his voice.

She was held captive for five terror-filled days until she miraculously escaped. Her kidnapper was arrested and sentenced to life in prison.

When I heard her story, I apologized for not getting all those details. She told me, "I was happy you did not know all the information because I would have thought you saw me on television. I didn't want to live the awful details over again, but I did want the personal messages from my husband about his family." Then she asked me, "Why did I have to go through this?"

At that time I did not have an answer, but eventually, Debra took one of my workshops, and when I met her in person, I was able to receive information from my guides about some of her karmic lessons in this life. I was amazed by Debra's inner strength and psychic gifts. Her tragedy paved the way for the work her soul needs to do in this life. She is now actively helping other victims find their way.

* * *

Leah called me to ask if I could talk to her beloved husband, Abe. Leah was a very strong lady, and it was hard to believe she was in her eighties. She needed to tell her husband that she loved him. She needed her second chance to say goodbye.

I had barely started my meditation when I felt a sharp jolt of pain in my abdomen. The pain was very quick, and then it was over. I asked Leah, "I almost feel as if I have a bullet in my stomach. Is this your husband?"

Leah answered, "Yes, my husband was shot in the stomach. But his death was not quick. He lingered on the floor for a short time. I could have said goodbye, but instead, I thought he would live. I just knew he wouldn't leave me."

I told Leah, "I see an elderly gentleman. He is bald on the top of his head and doesn't seem very tall. But the funny thing is he is handing me a muffin. A muffin with black spots; it could be blueberries or raisins."

"Oh my God, that's Abe!" said Leah. "He was bald, and he wasn't very tall. And he ate a blueberry muffin for breakfast every morning for the last twenty years without fail."

"He is telling me that the pain was very quick. Even though he seemed to be lingering, he wasn't fully aware of the pain. He was focused on the sensation of his soul coming alive. The fluttering of his soul within his body was so powerful he couldn't feel the pain. When he finally passed, the light was so beautiful."

"Oh, Abe, I can't wait to be with you," Leah said. "The reason I am here today is because I want you to know how much I love you. Through the years we never talked about our love. We worked side by side, raised a family, but we never put our feelings into words." She sighed.

"He is telling me to thank you for being his partner. He loves you, and you both will be together again. You have a little more time on Earth."

"Now I am seeing a cash register. I see a young man, confusion, and I feel the impact and a bang. Does this make sense to you?"

"We had a little grocery store in our old neighborhood," she said. "I told Abe we should close the store because the area was changing, but he loved his store. We were robbed several times before. This night, we were just about to close the store when two boys entered, one waving a gun and demanding money from the cash register. Abe was about to give the young man the money. I guess one boy panicked. He shouted, 'He's got a gun!' I tried to tell him that we didn't have a gun, but it happened so fast. Abe was shot in his stomach." Leah sobbed, "Why did this happen to him? He was such a good man. He helped everyone."

Abe interrupted, and I told Leah, "He wants me to explain that his soul agreed to atone for the injustice he caused in another life. In that life he preyed on young boys and abused them sexually. Then he killed them so they could not identify him in the village. He went to his soul review when he died. He felt their pain, but it wasn't enough. He chose to come back to Earth and die by his victim's hand. He asks you to remember when our son was molested at knifepoint as a child. Abe had to endure the same pain as the parents of his victims. Even though your son was not killed, Abe experienced what it felt like to be unable to save a child from harm."

He continued to tell me that his soul review this time was pleasant. He saw the times he had helped people make positive changes in their lives. He was a loving husband, father and grandfather. He also helped neighborhood teenagers when they were in trouble.

"He wants you to know he is at peace. Goodbye for now."

I watched as Abe stepped back to my gatekeeper and faded from my sight.

When I last heard from Leah, her health was failing, and she was waiting in peace to join Abe.

* * *

A friend referred Marilyn to me with hopes that I could give her some answers. When I heard her son was involved in a murder and then killed himself, I asked her if I could tape this session for my book. She agreed, but when I reached her son Donald, he did not want to be part of the book. With the permission of his mother, I taped the session anyway. When I went to play back the tape, there was nothing on it. Donald got his way, but we eventually managed to persuade him to share his story in my book.

When I went into my trance, I saw an arrogant young man step forward and demand, "What do you want?" I also saw an elderly woman and felt chest pains. She was telling me, "mother."

Marilyn confirmed, "Yes, my mother had chest pains when she died."

Her mother added, "Even though I died before Donald was born, I have always been close to him. I was with him when he crossed over to the other side."

Next, a balding man pushed forward and said to me, "What about my heart? I had a heart attack. Doesn't anyone remember my heart attack?"

I described the man to Marilyn. She told me this was her dead husband. "I don't want to speak to him. Go away, you bastard!" she yelled.

Her husband said, "Oh, now you're getting riled!"

I realized this was nonproductive, so I ignored the man. He was obviously a soul who chose to stay stuck in his ego.

Donald seemed wary of me as he asked with a calmer voice, "What do you want? How can I help you?"

Marilyn answered, "I just want to know that you are all right."

I told Marilyn that he was sympathetic toward her as he answered, "Mom, I'm fine."

She asked, "Do you see Brenda?"

When I heard that question, I had an awful feeling that Brenda was the person he murdered. I heard the word "girlfriend." I asked, "Was Brenda his girlfriend, and is she the one he murdered?"

Marilyn answered, "Yes."

"He tells me he has seen Brenda. Their souls have worked things out. They are in different group souls because their lessons are different. He also tells me he is sorry for the pain he put you through. He and Brenda were having a lot of problems. That night they were arguing, and he started drinking which made his temper escalate.

"I see a fight now, and she is leaving the house. Does that make sense to you?"

"Yes," Marilyn told me. "She left to walk the dog."

"He is telling me that he was full of anger. The next thing he knew, he was out of control. He followed her and shot her. When he realized what he had done, he was afraid."

Marilyn agreed, "I'm sure."

"He wants you to know his mind was so confused. Then he knew he was looking down on his own body. At that point he realized he had killed himself. Now he knows it was all so wrong. He made the wrong choice, and now he has to deal with it."

"Are you in hell?" Marilyn's voice shook as she asked the question. "This is a great concern to me since you committed a murder."

"He is telling me, 'No, Mom. I will go to places of healing and learning. There are different degrees of murder. I did not sit and plan to kill anyone, and it was never my intention to do so. I am now learning with others who also acted impulsively.'" Then I continued, "Donald is saying these words to me, 'Mom, I finally feel like I belong somewhere.'"

Marilyn spoke softly, "I'm so happy, Donny. So you didn't suffer?"

"He is explaining to me that when he went to his soul review and watched his life, he felt pain. When he saw the pain he caused you and his sister, he truly suffered. He watched the heartache Brenda's family went through, and he suffered more. When he comes back to Earth, his new life will be harder. He says his road will be paved with retribution."

Marilyn added, "Relationships were always hard for you."

"He is talking about a sister. I think relationships are hard for both him and his sister."

Marilyn said, "That's right."

Donald's voice weakened as he said these words: "It started with Dad. The bad things he did when we were small. I'll never forgive myself for not helping my sister."

I did not understand what was being said, but Marilyn was in agreement. She said, "I found out later what that bastard did to your sister. I'm so sorry. If I had known, I would have done something."

"Donald is telling me that his father was the root of all his problems. His father is stuck, even in spirit. He doesn't want to heal, but he has free will, and his guides will help him when he wants to change."

I listened to Donald, then I said, "He is ready to heal. He has found love there, and he's bonded with others, but his stay there is temporary. He will return to Earth someday and learn the lessons he refused to learn the last time around. It will take him time to build the strength he will need for the next life. He loves you and hopes his story can help."

Marilyn answered, "I love you, Donny."

He looked into my eyes with remorse and said, "I have to go now."

I thanked him, and he was gone.

Marilyn now had the understanding she needed to heal. Healing has been a hard process for her. As she explained, there are plenty of support groups for the family of victims, but when you're the mother of a murderer, you don't know where to go. In her daily life old acquaintances did everything they could to avoid her. She did not raise her son to kill someone; it just happened. Now she has to live with the pain of losing a son and the guilt of loving a murderer.

Marilyn told me that after her chance to say goodbye, her healing has begun.

* * *

I answered my telephone for my nine o'clock appointment. A young man introduced himself as Tony, age twenty-seven. His voice was very quiet, and he seemed unsure of himself. He told me that his mother had died recently, and he wanted to know if she was all right. I told him that I could not call a particular spirit, but we'd see what happens.

I closed my eyes, said a prayer and began to meditate. The spirit of a woman showed herself to me, but she seemed very young. I told Tony, "I see a young woman. She seems to be in her forties. She's thin, her face is drawn and she looks very tired. I think life was hard for her."

"Yes, that's my mom," he answered. "Please tell her I'm sorry she was alone."

"She is telling me it wasn't your fault," I said. "Now I am being shown an image. I see a small room with no furniture. I feel very confined in this room. Does that make sense to you?"

"Yes," Tony answered.

"I sense this has to do with her death. You wanted to be with her, but for some reason you could not."

"Yes," Tony responded sadly. "I feel bad that she was all alone when she died. I wanted to be there, but I was in jail. I just got out after being locked up for a year."

"She is telling me that she had been alone all her life, and she was alone at her death," I said. "I feel pains in my stomach. Did your mother have stomach problems?"

"I'm not sure. She didn't have insurance, so she saw doctors in many different clinics which made it hard for me to get any answers. The hospital told me that the cause of death was internal bleeding. They may have mentioned her stomach. I know she wasn't taking care of herself."

"She wants to leave now," I said. "Her soul is very tired. She wants me to tell you she loves you." I paused before continuing. "As she is leaving, I can see a spirit of a man. He has long, dark, wavy hair. I think he is in his late twenties, but it seems he lived a very hard life. He is showing me beads. They are black and gold."

Tony's voice was very surprised as he answered me. "Yes, that's my brother Rico. He was in a gang called the Latin Kings in New York. All the gang members wore black and gold beads!"

"I feel an impact to my back," I said. "Did something happen to that part of his body?"

"He was shot in the back," said Tony. "Murdered."

"Rico wants me to ask you to help him," I said. "I think he did very bad things to people when he was alive, and he is having a hard time on the other side."

"How can I help him when I can't even help myself?" Tony asked.

"He is telling me, 'It is not your time. Go back to school. Get a degree in social work. This way you can help guys like us. They will listen to you. My spirit will work by your side. This will help my karma.' Do you understand?" I asked.

Tony sat quietly for a moment, then asked, "What is karma?"

"Karma is the law of cause and effect. When you do wrong to yourself or anyone else, you have to correct that wrong by doing good. If you don't, your soul is the victim of retribution," I explained. "Does that make sense?"

"Yes," he said and proceeded to share his thoughts with me. "I was going to kill myself. I just got out of jail. My life had no purpose. But now if Rico will help me, I can try to do this. I do want to help him."

"You're his last link with life," I said. "You can help his soul by doing good for others."

Tony thanked me and promised he would not try to kill himself. Rico disappeared and our session ended.

* * *

During one of my readings, a young girl named Kara sat at my table. She gave me a smile and said she wanted to talk to Chuck. I closed my eyes, said my prayer and went into my meditation. The spirit of a young man with a mischievous grin told me he was Chuck.

I asked Kara if it was a romantic relationship as I felt a strong pull of love between them.

"Yes," she answered.

I then felt pains in my chest, and the end seemed to come in an instant. "Was his death quick?" I asked. "Was it an accident?"

"Yes," she said again.

Then I felt as if my chest exploded, and I thought Chuck must have had a heart attack. I shared these sensations with Kara.

"It wasn't a heart attack," she said, "but his heart did explode. He was shot in the chest."

I asked her if she knew what had happened because it seemed to me that Chuck needed to explain his death to her. Kara told me she did not know how he died but really needed to find out.

"I am feeling he was outside by his car," I began. "He is showing me someone stopping his car. He stopped to see what was wrong. You don't believe it was a robbery, do you?"

"No," Kara answered.

"He is telling me it started out to be a robbery, but something went wrong, and he was shot."

"So he wasn't buying drugs?" Kara asked.

Chuck told me to tell her, "You don't really believe that."

"No," she said, sadly. "But what was he doing in the center of Philadelphia?"

"He tells me he was looking to buy something for his computer."

"He did work with computers," said Kara.

I explained to her he is very happy that she doesn't believe he was buying drugs because his family thinks that is how he died. She nodded in agreement. "He wants you to know he is so sorry he left you so soon. It seems you liked him first. He is glad that you came on to him. Since you didn't have much time together, I'm feeling you met at work. Did you work together?"

She looked at me very surprised and started to laugh. "That was an ongoing joke between us—the night I met him, I gave him a big kiss on the mouth. We didn't work together, but I was introduced to him at my job."

"Now he is talking to me about the wedding," I said. "I feel you both were in the midst of planning it."

"Today was supposed to be our wedding day," she answered, her eyes filling with tears.

"He is asking me if you would do him a favor. He asks me to tell you that he wants to hold you again. Tonight, sit in meditation and allow his spirit to touch your spirit."

Kara asked me how to do this, and I told her how to sit quietly, focus on her breathing and stay relaxed until his spirit enters into her energy field. I told her that she would feel sensations in her body such as warmth, tingling and light touches.

Kara agreed, and we said our goodbyes. I trust that she made a peaceful connection to the one she loved that night and found the healing that would allow her to move on.

* * *

I sat in my meditation and prayer. As I focused, I could see a man, tall and thin, who had experienced a long, drawn-out illness. I could feel his death was fairly recent. Barbara agreed that this was a clear description of her husband, Jack. Then the spirit of a woman came into my vision.

"She is telling me, 'mother,'" I said.

"Yes," said Barbara, "my mother is dead. She has been gone for a long time."

"I am feeling pain in the back of my head," I continued. "I also feel she was confused when she died. Does that make sense to you?"

"Absolutely," Barbara answered. "She was drunk at the time of her death."

"Was your mother murdered?" I asked.

"I believe so. The police said she fell and bumped her head, but how could she fall backwards behind her television? It never felt right to me," Barbara explained.

"She is saying, 'boyfriend.' Did she have a boyfriend?"

"No, not that I know of," said Barbara.

"Now she is showing me a man, a man she might have met when she was in a bar while picking up packaged beer. Did she ever pick up strange men?" I asked.

"She sure did," Barbara confirmed.

"Well, that's what happened," I said. "He came over to drink with her, and she became drunk and nasty. They started fighting. Now she is showing me that she fumbled with her money; he grabbed her pocketbook, and she chased after him. He pushed her, she lost her balance and fell backward to the floor. She died immediately. I don't think it was his intention to kill her. It seemed like an accident."

Barbara sighed. "That makes sense because it was the first of the month, and she had just received her checks. I always knew there was some kind of foul play even if the police did not believe me. Please ask her why her place was so neat. It was never that clean when she drank."

"Your mother is telling me she straightened up the place before her friend came over. But now I am seeing a man taking out a bag of garbage. That's strange. Why would he kill her and then clean her apartment?" I wondered aloud.

Barbara answered, "He obviously didn't want anyone to know someone had been in the house with her. How did he leave her apartment?"

"She is telling me, 'Out the back.' Do you understand that?" I asked.

"Yes," said Barbara, "I always had a hunch that the person went out the back bathroom window. The doors to her apartment were locked from the inside, so the police believed she was drunk and fell. But I knew there was more. I thought it might have been one of her neighbors who always seemed suspicious to me. Someone stole her belongings before I got there," she explained.

"From what your mother is showing me, it was a man," I said. "She is giving me the word 'disability.' A man on disability."

"That neighbor was on disability," said Barbara. "Was it the neighbor or the man from the bar?"

"I don't know," I said. "She is starting to fade."

"At least I know I was right, and my mother was murdered, even if it was unintentional and the result of a fight," said Barbara.

"Before she goes, she wants you to know how much she loved you," I said. "She is sorry for all the pain she put you through when you lived with her. She had a hard time understanding you, but in her own way she always loved you. She had a lot of problems that prevented her from being the mother you deserved. Now she is showing me your home. I see a bathtub in the kitchen."

"Yes, we did have two tubs attached to the sink."

After a moment of silence, Barbara added, "I know she loved me; I just feel bad that she had such a wasted life."

"She wants you to know she was ready to move into spirit, and she is at peace now," I explained.

Barbara sighed once again. "After hearing the news of mom's death, I flew immediately to her town. That night, I slept in her apartment on the couch. It took me a long time to fall asleep because I kept trying to figure out how she died. When I had finally fallen asleep, I was awakened by a touch to my face. It felt like a kiss on my check. Then I heard my mother's voice telling me to forget it, that it was an accident."

Even though all of Barbara's questions were not answered, she now knows her mother truly wants her to let it go. It was her mother's fate to die as she did.

* * *

Kathleen called at her appointed time, and my guide Great White Spirit and I prepared for the reading. I said my prayers and began my meditation. There were several spirits waiting, but an elderly woman approached my guide and said something to him. She was allowed through first.

She told me, "I am her maternal grandmother. Remind her of all the happy times we spent together during her younger years."

"Yes, that's grandma. Tell her I remember," Kathleen said.

Then a young girl appeared to me. I heard, "age eighteen." She was very pretty and had an upbeat personality. I felt the connection was that of a daughter.

I hesitated and asked, "Where is your daughter?"

"She is dead," Kathleen replied.

Then I described the girl I was seeing, and Kathleen's voice cracked. "Yes, that is my Lisa."

Lisa did not want to wait for an introduction. She blurted out to me, "Even though my murder was brutal, I felt no pain." She was showing me a scene outside. She took me closer, and I saw bones scattered around. I shook my head to clear it because I didn't want to see more. I told Kathleen what I saw, and she confirmed that it was the crime scene. She asked, "Lisa, what happened?"

"Lisa is telling me she took a chance with a man she did not know."

Kathleen admonished, "Talking is one thing. Getting into a vehicle with a stranger is another."

"She is telling me she had done it many times before. She seems to have been the type of person who was completely wrapped up in herself. She is sorry for not taking the time to understand you."

Kathleen sounded resigned when she replied, "It was her age. I understand that."

I tried to be gentle when I said, "She didn't want to be like you."

Kathleen replied, "I understand that too."

There was a long pause, and then Lisa asked me to ask her mother if she remembered how much she liked children.

"Yes," Kathleen replied.

Lisa went on to tell me that the place she was in was great and that she wanted her mother to know that she now works with children. When she is not in her group soul, she is working with these joyful souls. She added that she knows she wasn't an easy child to raise.

When I had told Kathleen all that Lisa said, Lisa abruptly changed the subject. "Now she is telling me something about horses," I said. "I think the reason she likes horses so much is that she felt like a wild horse herself. She wanted to run and be free. She is explaining that she sometimes felt trapped inside her body. She wanted to do more to grow up fast. Now she is finally at peace."

Then I saw a pony step in and stand beside Lisa. "Did she have a pony?" I asked.

Kathleen answered, "Yes."

I described the pony to Kathleen, and she said, "Yes, that was Lisa's first pony. She loved him dearly. The pony died shortly after Lisa."

Lisa told me she is so happy to be with her pony. "Lisa feels your horse might also be with her soon," I said.

Kathleen agreed, saying, "The horse's problems are getting worse."

"She is now telling me the word 'divorce.' I'm sorry, but she's fading in and out, and I can't get the rest."

"My divorce was very hard for her," Kathleen said.

"Well, she understands that now," I said.

"Does she have any advice for me?" Kathleen asked.

Lisa answered quickly. I listened and tried to repeat all her words. "You don't hold me back and you don't pull me down. You are fully accepting. I am so glad you're getting on with your life. However, you don't have a relationship right now. I feel you have built a wall around yourself. You need to stop and allow yourself to be loved. You deserve it."

"You told her you left your husband because you wanted happiness," I continued. "Now you have peace of mind, but you don't have happiness. She wants you to let someone love you."

"You know," Kathleen said to Lisa, "I've been giving that a lot of thought lately. I realize that I feel unworthy of happiness. I left you and your brother with your father, Lisa, and I guess I should not have done that."

"Now she is saying, 'forgiveness,'" I told Kathleen. "She is telling me that when you get to this side, you will have a soul review, sort of a judgment day without judgment. You are responsible for loving and taking care of yourself first, then family, then community. You can't truly love anyone until you love yourself. Then love can radiate from within to others. Look at everything that is wonderful about you. Now you need love in your life."

A deep sigh came from Kathleen, and she said, "Yes."

Lisa continued, "It is time for you to trust again."

Kathleen agreed again, "Yes, trust is a huge issue right now. I'm so used to people leaving me."

"Lisa is telling me she learned that you don't have control of anyone. Just take each day as it comes. Nothing on Earth is forever. Embrace the moment and be happy."

Kathleen whispered an emotional, "Thank you."

"Lisa needs to leave now," I said.

"Can she please stay a little longer?" Kathleen asked.

I explained, "She is with you. The old relationship is gone, and you have both been healed. Now it's time for your spiritual relationship to begin."

CHAPTER 8

Animals and the Afterlife

Animals are so important in our lives. Not only do they give us companionship, but in many cases they bring healing to our souls. They teach us how to love unconditionally. It never surprises me when I am in a session with a client and an animal spirit pops its head into the vision just to say "hi" to its companion. Sometimes it doesn't matter how long the animal has been in spirit; it is still watching over and loving its person.

Many times clients call me for a reading and apologize for sounding stupid because they want to speak to a pet who has passed to the other side. It is far from silly. We have suffered a loss and go through the same grieving process we would in the death of anyone we love.

I introduced my Siamese cat Tiki in Chapter 1. He was my best friend and confidante all of his life, and I loved him. I could tell him my problems and fears, and he would snuggle in my arms and let me know that he was there for me. His love for me was unconditional. He didn't care how I looked, what I wore or what I said; he just loved me. Everyone who has had a pet knows how this feels.

Tiki was with me for nineteen years through thick and thin, and then he started to fail. His decline took about one year. He became disoriented and howled a lot in his confusion. Tiki's weight dropped dramatically from his already lean body, and it was painful to watch him wasting away. I was pregnant with Sarah, and he made it clear to me in our unspoken language that he wanted to be with me when she was born.

Shortly after Sarah's birth, Tiki became incoherent and would stand in a corner and howl at the top of his lungs. He would sometimes shriek all night long. I was already exhausted from my pregnancy, Sarah's birth and the schedule of the infant, so this was a terrible situation for all of us. My daughter was finally sleeping through the night, but my cat was keeping me awake. Lucas and I took turns trying to keep him calm and take care of Sarah. It was a very difficult time of my life, to say the least.

I called Anita, the animal communicator, and we questioned Tiki to see if he was ready to move on in his spiritual journey, and he assured us that he was. He felt uncomfortable in his body and was unhappy about his state of confusion. Tiki told us that he had some medical problems coming up in the near future if he stayed around, and he would not mind missing the pain that those problems would bring. He had lingered here to make contact with Sarah and was pleased with that meeting, but now he was annoyed by her presence and wanted more time with me. He knew that his thoughts were irrational, but he could not help feeling that way. He said he wanted to leave and could be more useful from the other side.

Within a few weeks Tiki's kidneys and liver started to shut down. He was obviously in pain and very disoriented. He was howling non-stop by then, and our neighbors were starting to wonder what was going on in our apartment. I put Tiki in the cat carrier and went to the vet with Lucas and my friend Andrea. He agreed that it was time to put Tiki down. However, Tiki, with a burst of energy, took off and raced around the office. When I caught him, he fought with all of his might which was considerable for the condition he was in. I was sobbing. I didn't know if this six-pound tiger wanted to stay or go, but I decided to let him go. The veterinarian had told us to take time with Tiki to say goodbye, but I was so upset I couldn't do it. How do you say goodbye and put a lethal needle into the vein of someone you have loved and nurtured for twenty years? Tiki's eyes were vacant, and he looked at me without recognition, but I still felt like I was letting him down.

Tiki fought the needle as much as he had fought being in the office, but finally it was over. Lucas had put a pillow under his head to make him comfortable. I was devastated and uncertain about my decision, but it could not be reversed. Lucas drove me home, and I sat down to calm myself. Something caught my eye, and as I turned to focus better, I saw Tiki walking across the room. He looked young and healthy, and his tail was up. I realized that I had not seen his tail up, as a healthy cat's would be, for a very long time.

My tears stopped flowing, and I was able to say goodbye to the Tiki I once knew, the healthy Tiki of the past. I knew I could call him to me at any time, and he would come. One day he will return to me in a new healthy body, and we will once again snuggle.

It is much easier for animals to move in and out of the spiritual realm since they don't have the karma that we do. They are born to give us love and to show us love. They have jobs with us, such as protector or companion. If they become mean, it is because a human taught them to be that way. This karma is on the human, not the animal.

When it is the animal's time to leave its physical body, it does so. The pet doesn't have a problem with letting go of a body that does not work anymore. His instinct is to find a quiet place where he cannot be seen and allow his soul to gently leave his body. In nature a predator would probably find the dying animal and kill it quickly, eliminating a prolonged period of suffering. The wild animals accept this system and are comfortable with it. Even though pets have been domesticated from their wild ancestors for a relatively short number of years, their end comes in a different manner. They don't feel the freedom to just go and die. The pet feels a bond with his person, and he worries about his person being able to cope with his death when he leaves. It may not be a possibility for the pet to just disappear. Therefore, the person might have to make a decision to either euthanize or allow the animal to die naturally. This sometimes leads to guilt either way. In any session where I had an animal that was euthanized or had some pain before he left his body on his own, the animal was fine with the decision that was made. The pet knew the choice was made out of love and supported the choice.

When I was thirteen, my childhood dog, Skippy, was eighteen years old. That was quite old, even for a Toy Fox Terrier. He was ill, and he needed medication to stay alive. My mother always tied him right outside our door. He would bark when he was done with his business and wanted to come in. One day we heard no barking. Skippy's rope was untied, and he was gone.

My mother searched the neighborhood day in and day out. She put ads in the paper and on the radio. We couldn't understand where he could have gone. He could hardly walk, but he had just disappeared.

Weeks went by, and my mother sat by the window crying. The most difficult part of Skippy's disappearance was that she needed closure. My pain was very strong, but this dog was another child to my mother.

My mother had a dream that my aunt, who was in spirit, came to her holding Skippy. He was all white and he looked young again. Then she knew he was at peace.

* * *

Jenny loved her Yorkshire Terrier, Violet. She called me for a session with her grandmother but also hoped that Violet would contact her. Jenny had many dogs in her life, but Violet was very special.

I closed my eyes, said my prayer and began my meditation. There was a very small dog looking at me. I could see something wrong with one of her eyes. I asked, "Was she blind in one eye?"

Jenny gasped, "Yes, she was."

"She has a very cute face. It almost looks as if she is smiling. Does that make sense to you?" I asked.

Jenny answered, "She always looked as if she was smiling." Jenny was delighted to feel Violet's presence in our session, but she was anxious to know if Violet would come back to her. She longed to hold her again.

Violet told me to tell Jenny she is ready to come back, but Jenny is not ready for her. Jenny sounded surprised, "What does she mean, I am not ready for her?"

"I'm sorry," I said. "She doesn't think you are. She is telling me you need to concentrate on finding a partner. You are lonely and deserve to have human companionship."

Jenny replied, "I do want to get married and have a family, but I keep meeting the wrong men. I'm in my forties now. It just seems impossible."

"Violet wants you to know it's not impossible. She can help you from the other side. She assures me you will get married and have a child, and she will come back to you as your family dog after your baby is born."

Jenny sighed, "It all sounds so wonderful. I hope you are right."

Violet told me to tell Jenny how much she loved her. She also said, "Remember, I will do my part in spirit if you do your part on Earth." Then Violet disappeared and was gone from my vision.

Before Jenny ended the call, she asked me what was her part and what she should do to help Violet. I told Jenny to be positive and believe it is going to happen. I gave her a soul mate meditation.

Jenny did that meditation religiously every night. She is married now and waiting for her baby to be born in a few months.

Soon Jenny and Violet will be together again.

* * *

A young lady named Megan called to set up an appointment. She told me she just wanted to know if her father was all right. He had died recently after a long illness, and she was worried about him, so we set up a session.

When she called, I opened with my meditation and a prayer. I felt the presence of Great White Spirit. I stared into my vast world of spirit to find her father.

The only spirit I could see was a small cat. It's hard for me to see colors of animals because they are all pure white light. However, I was getting the feeling this cat was gray striped. I tried to push the feeling away in order to contact Megan's father, but the cat kept coming back.

I told Megan, "I'm sorry, but I am not seeing a man. Oddly enough, I am seeing a cat. I think it has gray stripes. It seems like he had problems with his legs." I asked if that meant anything to her.

She answered, "Yes," very quietly.

I told her that I was feeling that the cat wanted me to tell her that he is okay. "I feel that you might have been worried about this cat." Megan suddenly started to cry uncontrollably. I waited for her to regain her composure and reassured her again that the cat was okay.

Megan explained, "My cat, Barry, was my best friend. I grew up with him. He was seventeen years old when I went to college. A few weeks after I left, my mother told me he was having trouble walking. He became insistent on going outside which was strange because for years he had been an inside cat. One day he sneaked out and was never seen again. I felt so guilty because I thought he was trying to find me. We looked all over but couldn't find him. I was so worried about him and thought I should have taken him to college with me. This guilt has been tearing me apart for years." Her sobbing increased.

I went back in to see if I could get another message from her cat. Barry was ready to try to help Megan through her grief. I told her, "Barry is now telling me that his job was done. He helped raise you and was your best friend, and then his time here was finished. His body was old and tired. He waited for you to leave for college, and then he went to find his very own place to die. He is now young and healed. He will watch over you from the heavenly realm. In time, when you are settled, he will find a new body and become your cat again." Then he was gone.

I apologized to Megan for not connecting with her father. She told me she loved her father very much, but seeing Barry again was what she needed in order to heal. As I started to close, I saw her father smiling as he held Barry in his arms.

If you have lost your pet, allow yourself to grieve. Animals are a very special part of our universe. Many people need the unconditional love of a pet to survive the rigors of life and stay healthy. Animals are continuous beings of love that travel with you to love you and help you get through the bumpy road of life.

Part Three

Receiving Peace

Death is both dramatic and subtle. Over time, the parting of a loved one becomes less harsh as slowly and gently a continued bond is revealed. As I open my heart to the promptings and guidance of those I love who have passed from the physical sphere, I am alert to the contact which comes to me in many forms—as memory, as intuition and coincidence. Rather than bitterly close my heart, I allow myself to maintain a gentle but alert attention to the touch of Spirit. I remind myself that life begats life and that those I love live on in my loving memory of them. I also allow for the possibility that my memory lives on in them, triggering their concerned contact in subtle forms. "Today, I deliberately practice open-mindedness. I cultivate a willingness to experience subtle realms."

--Julia Cameron
Transitions

CHAPTER 9

Glimpses of the Other Side

A second chance to say goodbye is saying goodbye to the physical relationship. The former connection was with the person you knew in a physical body and with whom you will now come to know in a new soul relationship.

I opened this book with the story of how I found my relationship with my soul. Once I found this, I was able to connect with the souls around me. Think of a soul as the most positive, loving force that lives deep within each person. Not his face, not his reputation, but the light that lives deep inside.

Every person has a glimmer of light within. However, it may be obscured by fear and ego. Most of the time, we don't focus on letting this light shine. We clutter our minds with material thoughts. We worry about the past and are anxious about the future. To understand the condition of the departed soul in relation to its loved ones still on Earth, make an analogy between our bodies and our homes. Usually, people live in several different houses during their lifetimes. They develop relationships while in one place and begin new relationships when they move. The relationships they had in their old home may change, but the ties still remain. In other words the soul may leave its house (body), but the ties to loved ones and sometimes enemies still remain.

No matter how many homes we live in, each relationship we share while living in these homes has a lasting impact on our life. Some relationships are stronger than others, and the love from these relationships remains with us throughout our lives. For example, when our children leave home for college, they begin new relationships. The ties they had with their parents change, but the connection is still there even though their homes have changed. Dying is a similar situation. Our soul moves through many bodies or lives which in theory are like our houses. However, the relationships we shared throughout these lives with our loved ones never die.

Spend some time in contemplation. Go deep within yourself, beyond your ego, beyond your belief system and test your soul. This part of you is what will communicate with your loved one. Your belief system is part of your rational, thinking mind. Your soul transcends this limited aspect of your mind. This is the way it is supposed to be, a connection from soul to soul. Once you can experience your soul, you will feel your departed loved one's soul around you. In Chapter 13, I describe a meditation that explains what it feels like to die. This meditation brings you deep within yourself so you can feel your soul. Once you can feel your soul, the connection with your loved one is a natural state. The former physical life of that person is no longer relevant.

Understanding death helps get rid of the fear that surrounds it. According to surveys, when people are asked what they fear most, the number one answer given is death. The second is the fear of the unknown. Therefore, if you get rid of the uncertainty death represents, it becomes easier to relate to your loved one. Death can be compared to taking a wonderful trip. It is hard for you to relate to it because you never took this trip before. When the deceased shares information of his experience, your new relationship will begin. Now you can relate to his soul. Your life will also become more fulfilling as you are adding a new dimension to it. You will then learn to enjoy your life in your physical body. When you can feel your soul within, you will realize that you are an eternal part of the universe.

Through many years of doing this work, I have pieced together the complexity of death. The guides and spirits I communicate with as a medium have helped me understand the process a soul goes through. The process is called death.

As the moment of death approaches, the physical body starts to become acutely aware of all of its senses. Familiar sensations intensify—the way the room feels, the sounds in the distance, even the smells that fill the room. These are the senses functioning in their natural state. Through the years they become dull because our mind becomes overloaded with the thoughts of worry and fear. At the time of death, our senses start to peak. The focus is then pulled into the center. Deep inside this center, one feels a flickering sensation. The connection with the body and soul has been made. The feeling of this connection is wonderful as the focus is now on the soul. The physical body starts to feel heavy and dense. The physical body is pulled in deeper by the Earth's gravitational force and takes its last breath as the soul rises above the body and says its farewell. If death occurs suddenly, the flickering is felt outside the body.

A person's belief system at the time of death will determine who will meet the soul after death and how it will enter the new dimension or plane. For example, loved ones, angels, spirit guides, a beloved pet or a revered religious figure may meet and guide the soul. The soul may also see a light, be drawn through a tunnel or feel a gravitational pull as he enters the astral realm which is a vibratory frequency rather than a place. The soul is housed in several bodies: the physical, mental, astral and spiritual. The physical body lives on the Earth plane. When we see our loved one die, we are seeing the death of the physical body. However, the other bodies live on, housing the soul.

The mental body is our thought system. Remember, the brain has died inside the physical body, but the mental body moves on with the same thoughts one has had. If one is at peace with oneself at the time of death, the peace remains with the soul. If he is in turmoil, the turmoil stays with him. The turmoil is temporary; the soul eventually finds peace. When I communicate with a soul who has just died and again a year later, the change is amazing.

The astral body then moves into the astral world. This body is in perfect condition. For instance, anyone who is blind or deaf, in a wheelchair or has experienced a disease that left the body in a deteriorated condition will no longer take his disabilities with him into the spirit realm. At times a spirit appears to me with a visible physical defect; this is only presented so that the spirit can be recognized by the loved one who wishes to contact him.

In many ways the astral world is as real as the physical Earth. It is an etheric counterpart to Earth. This invisible world extends around the Earth and is composed of astral energy that vibrates at frequencies beyond the physical plane. It looks and feels like Earth but is minus physical pain. This eases the shock of leaving the solid, physical world and allows the spirit to slide slowly into the afterlife. Within a short time the astral body dissolves, and the soul moves to the heavenly realm in its spiritual body.

The soul experiences a soul review in this dimension. This is the place where the soul's actions on Earth are evaluated without judgment. During this review the soul experiences the joy it brought to each person and also feels the accumulated pain of each person it has hurt. As you dwell there, each aspect of your life on Earth is discussed.

An etheric council will decide what was accomplished on Earth and what is needed for the soul to progress. The etheric council is a group of highly evolved beings who have completed their earthly incarnations. A religious person may see Jesus at the head of the assembly. The recommendations they give you will decide what group soul you will occupy.

After the soul review the soul moves to a healing chamber where it is nurtured and healed in a pool of thick, warm, green mist. Memories of pain and unhappiness from Earth that linger in the mental body are healed so that peace is restored to the soul. Most materialistic memories are now dissolved.

My father dwelled in the healing chamber about two years of Earth time. He suffered from illness for years on the Earth plane. When his physical body died, it was very deteriorated, so he needed rest. Since time does not exist in this dimension, things seem to move very quickly there.

Next, the soul will move on to a place where it is part of a spiritual family where all members learn to understand the full essence and capabilities of the soul. Spirit guides form a bond with the group and play an instrumental part in each soul's life. There is no need to express thoughts and feelings verbally in this heavenly atmosphere because spirits in this dimension are telepathic. Our thoughts and feelings can be hidden while we are on Earth, but here every thought is part of the spirit, and it appears as its own individual light. Each soul incorporates all of its earthly experiences and personalities into oneness with God. The souls are now part of Unconditional Love.

Souls who have chosen to commit negative actions on Earth are placed in a group soul with other souls who made the same choices. They are instructed with lessons of love.

Ego ceases to exist here. The thoughts and fears of materialism are washed away. This is why when a loved one is in spirit for a long period of time, it is difficult to get specific details. They no longer relate to the solid vibrations of Earth. They are still connected with you through love but not by material things. This is where the soul will stay until it is reunited with its loved ones who are still on the Earth plane. These souls will help their loved ones ascend into the heavenly realm when they die.

While your loved one is progressing in the group soul, he can feel you thinking of him. He will feel your longing and come to your side. Love can penetrate through different dimensions. It is very important to work on keeping your thought system positive since the soul of your loved one can hear you. I know your grief is very strong and sometimes hard to deal with, but remember, he is on the other side and still loving you. He does not want to see you experiencing pain. Remember the story of the little boy who told his mother that he was afraid to communicate with her because he would make her cry. Every time she thought of him, she was sad, and he wanted to see her happy again.

Spirits really do want to help and comfort you. They want to stop your pain, but when you feel despair, they feel helpless.

The first thing you need to do is to work on yourself. Let your loved one go for a while. He is working on his progression in the heavenly realm. He is getting used to dwelling in pure love. By working through your stages of grief, you will find your way to acceptance.

Acceptance will come and go as you work through your grief. On the days when you feel acceptance, you can start to build a new relationship with the soul of your loved one. This is a very exciting process. Knowing that you and your loved one can still share special moments and knowing that the love between you will never die is a wonderful and joyous experience.

But first, let's work on finding acceptance.

CHAPTER 10

Transforming Grief into Peace

Arriving at the stage of acceptance is a process. Don't be afraid to grieve. Allow yourself to go through the five stages of grief as defined by Elizabeth Kübler Ross as denial, anger, bargaining, depression and acceptance.

Denial: An often-used defense mechanism that attempts to block out information that the psyche finds too overwhelming to accept.

Anger: An emotional response to the overwhelming "unfairness" of the circumstances.

Bargaining: Often shows up as an attempt to strike a deal with God. Bargaining can also be with oneself. For example: If I give up my own happiness, it will relieve me of guilt.

Despair/Depression: A prelude to acceptance. At this stage reality is dawning, yet emotional suffering is still acute.

Acceptance: Reconciliation to the new reality of moving forward in life without the physical presence of the person who has died.

These stages can help you work through this time of pain. They don't necessarily come into your life in any particular order. You may experience some of them, or your emotions may jump from stage to stage.

What you need to avoid is getting locked in any one stage for a long period of time. When the grieving process is prolonged, your connection with the other side might not happen. Your own ability to think clearly is stifled.

When my brother, Neil, died, I wanted to continue my life as it was, but his death changed everything. My life was never going to be the same. Everyone around me was overwhelmed with their own pain. Since I was five years old, no one thought I needed to be heard. They thought I couldn't understand.

My sister married when I was seven years old. She wanted to escape the unhappy household and work on her grief. I displaced my anger and directed it toward my sister. I was jealous. She was in another state, beginning a happy family life. My mother was working through her grief, but sadness still permeated our home. She had hung a large portrait of Neil which dominated the living room and kept his memory alive. I searched for peace but could find only anger.

When I was eighteen, I went to visit Neil's grave. I threw myself on the ground and cried, telling him I wasn't angry anymore. I had now accepted my anger, but I immediately went into the stage of bargaining. "Now that I've forgiven you," I cried, "please let me be happy." I was totally irrational. I bargained for a few minutes and expected to find happiness at once. As a result, the sadness was more intense, and I felt no communication from him whatsoever. Even if he had been trying to communicate with me, I would not have heard him because my mind was so busy with chatter and confusion.

I went into the stage of depression which eventually led to my suicide attempt. This led me to a counselor. I was so stuck in depression that I needed professional help.

It is very easy to get lost in one of these stages, and sometimes family members or friends are not able to help you. They just don't know what to say and are afraid of upsetting you.

During many years of doing this work, I have felt much pain from others. Most of my clients are people who are overwhelmed by one or more of these five stages of grief. I can only give them temporary relief—an understanding of death, a moment of connection. But when the session is over, they continue to live with their grief.

I began to realize the need for a special workshop, a place where people who are suffering from death can join together. They would be able to learn where they are in the stages of grief and how to understand the process of death. They could then transform their grief so they could start to have a new relationship with their loved one's soul. I created a unique workshop called "A Second Chance to Say Goodbye."

During the first half of the workshop, I explain how the soul processes death. I then connect with the spirits of the loved ones on the other side and teach the participants how to feel their presence. My goal is to help them discover what their loved ones are doing and feeling. With this new understanding they can move towards acceptance.

As I begin to teach the students what it feels like to have their own communication with their loved ones, I can feel a strong pull, as the spirits are anxious to express themselves. They know I am the link to their loved ones. I ask people to sit in a circle. I start with a prayer of protection and ask the spirits who are available to come into our space. Then I take the class through the "Meditation for Communication" found in Chapter 13. This opens them up to the spiritual realm, raising their vibrations so they can communicate themselves. As they are meditating, I can see the visiting spirits standing next to them. Each person can see the spirits in their meditation. This is a visitation.

Kimi was an attractive, thin woman, eager to talk to the spirits. As I entered into her energy field, I saw a young woman standing behind her.

"I feel a young woman's presence," I said. "She is telling me the word 'mother.' I feel there was trauma to her head."

The spirit came through more strongly. "She's telling me about an argument, one that took place between her and a man." Kimi confirmed that the man was her father. I felt the sensation of alcohol.

"Yes," Kimi said. "She and my father came home from a party."

"I feel a struggle. I feel her fall, and then I feel the trauma to her head," I told her. Kimi replied that she had been only one year old at the time of her mother's death. She had always known something violent had happened between her mother and father. She had only been told that her mother fell down the stairs and hit her head. Although she wasn't certain, she always felt that her father had been involved in her mother's death.

Her mother continued, "Tell Kimi how much I love her. I didn't want to leave my little girl. But I was there through every important moment of her life."

She goes on to tell her how sorry she was for all the hand-me-down clothes Kimi had to wear as a child. She wished she were there to buy her a beautiful dress. "Kimi I am so sorry for the pain you went through."

Kimi started to cry. "Yes, life with my father was very painful."

I helped Kimi go back to the meditation to feel her mother's presence and feel her mother's love around her. Then I moved to the next person.

Debbie was a woman in her forties. She had short blond hair and a pretty round face. When I looked in her eyes, I could visibly see the pain she was undergoing. "Who came to you?" I asked gently.

She bit her lower lip and held back her tears. "My husband. He came to me. I was really able to feel his presence and communicate with him."

I turned to her and smiled. "Yes, there is a man standing at your left side. Is that where you feel him?" I asked.

"Yes, he's touching my shoulder," Debbie said.

"He's a big man with a big smile and a good sense of humor. However, my head is filled with pain."

Tears rolled down her cheeks. "He died from brain cancer," Debbie confirmed.

I heard his voice in a rushed whisper. "He wants you to know that he is at peace, and the bond you share will be forever," I told her.

I moved to the next person, Amy. She was eagerly waiting to tell me about the presence of her mother. "I felt my mother sit next to me. It felt exactly like the times we spent having our long talks together," she said.

"You did well. There is a presence of a woman who had beautiful white wavy hair. She was about seventy years old," I said. "She wore glasses on the bridge of her nose and always peered over the top."

Amy gasped and said, "That's my mom!"

I felt a sharp pain stab throughout the area of my right breast as Amy's mother's face appeared. I could see her white hair clearly again. Amy covered her face with her hands and began to cry. "My mother had breast cancer, and her right breast was removed. She was upset because she lost her hair when she had chemotherapy."

I smiled at Amy and said, "Your mom is okay now."

Amy sighed, "That is just what I need to hear."

Dean and Mitzi sat in the far corner of the room. Mitzi was crying, and Dean was fighting back his tears.

I looked at them and asked, "Who did you see?"

To my surprise, Dean quickly responded, "My son! My son came to me!"

I glanced over to Mitzi, and she said, "I couldn't get anyone."

I looked into her eyes. "Your son is here," I explained. "He's standing between both of you."

"But why can't I feel him?" she asked.

"At this time your grief is too strong," I told her. "Give it time. Allow yourself to grieve." I sensed the presence of their son who apparently was a young man about twenty years old. "I feel an impact to my head," I said. "A quick death."

As the tears rolled down his face, Dean said, "He was twenty-one, and he was in a car accident. Please ask my son how it happened."

"Your son told me his vision was distracted by a box that he had in his car. He lost control of the car as a result."

"I really want to know if he felt any pain."

"No," I answered. "He was knocked out by the blow to his head."

His son went on to say, "Please stop fighting with each other. You need each other now. I love you both, and I will always be there for you."

Mitzi explained later that Jason had installed a new amplifier in his car that day, and he called it a box.

After I finished with all the people in the circle, I closed it by giving thanks to all the spirits that had come to help us on our path.

The students in this workshop realized that they could have some form of communication with their loved ones, and it was a welcome new beginning. They could take this meditation home and, on days when acceptance prevails, have their own personal communication.

Kimi was able to see that she had delayed her grief when she had gotten stuck in anger. Even though it had been many years since her mother's death, she realized that it was still possible to complete her grieving process and find her inner peace.

Debbie understood that she was in the stage of depression. By feeling her husband close to her again, she now realized the strong ties they once had were still there.

Once Amy knew her mother's suffering was over and she was at peace, Amy was able to resolve her feelings of despair. She felt acceptance.

Dean and Mitzi realized that the conflicts they experienced between them most often resulted from being in different stages of grieving. They were able to understand each other's pain more clearly and could now begin to compassionately support each other.

At times, acceptance will come and go. The stages change from moment to moment. You may even find yourself feeling guilty when you find acceptance, but eventually the acceptance stage will be with you more often.

Affirmations are a way of separating yourself from your grief. They can be powerful aids in helping you move through grief rather than remain stuck in it. These are some of the affirmations I use in my workshop:

Denial: I am in pain, and it's okay to feel pain. I choose to live in the joyful now.

Anger: I accept my feelings of anger, and I am able to forgive because I know my situation is no one's fault. Everything that happens is part of a divine plan.

Bargaining: I am strong and powerful. I am able to handle what happens in life. I accept the joy and challenges of life as it is.

Depression: I am connected to all living things. I am part of the cycle of life. All is well. I am loved.

Acceptance: At this moment, I accept my life as it is.

Put a list of the affirmations on the refrigerator door, on the wall, near the television or anywhere you can see it. Let the affirmations become a part of your life.

Some affirmations bring about a strong feeling of resistance. You need to explore that resistance to help yourself and to understand when you are at an impasse. If you are comfortable and have no resistance, move on to the next affirmation. The one that is the most difficult to affirm is probably the one you need the most.

One affirmation you can say immediately after a death is: "I am letting go. I have no control over this situation. I am okay."

Try to keep repeating these affirmations until you find comfort. There is no reason anyone needs to go through thirteen years of anger as I did.

CHAPTER 11

How Children Grieve

When the home is full of grief and adult emotions are out of control, children are often pushed aside. They become the silent grievers. Contrary to what many think during such a traumatic time, children can understand what is happening. No matter what the age, a child can feel the pain of the family. A child reacts to the parent's emotions even if the adult tries to cover and repress them. The healthiest way to help a child go through the grieving process is to take him aside and honestly share your feelings. Allow the child to ask you questions and be willing to answer them in a positive way. If you create a loving understanding of the child's feelings, he will know that he is allowed to grieve.

After the death of his grandmother, Joe told his mother that he felt very sad and that he couldn't stop crying. His mother told him it was okay to cry. Joe was the type of boy who needed structure from his mother, so he asked her how long he should cry. She told him that he would be able to stop in three days. He cried his eyes out for three days, and on the fourth day his tears stopped, and he was able to talk of the happy times he had spent with his grandmother. His mother had given him permission to grieve.

Caitlyn was six and her brother Patrick was five when their father died from cancer. Both children loved their father very much, but Caitlyn had a special attachment to him. They expressed their grief in very different ways. Caitlyn tried to deny her feelings completely and insisted on performing in her dance recital that was scheduled on the day her father died. Her mother, Patty, did not expect her to dance, but Caitlyn became very upset and could not understand her mother's reasoning. She danced that day.

Patrick expressed his grief by crying, whereas Caitlyn would not cry. She became very angry. She even acted cruelly to children around her. She would become angry with her brother when he cried or when he talked about his dad. The more her mother tried to have her express her feelings, the angrier Caitlyn became. She just wanted to be left alone.

As months went by, Patty became very concerned about her. She was amazed at the strength of her little girl but worried that she needed to express her feelings.

Patty quietly observed her. She realized that Caitlyn did not want to be different. Her daughter felt that everyone at school had a father, and this was a disturbing reality in her life. Caitlyn refused to discuss the subject with her mother. As time went by, Caitlyn remained caught in her grief, Patrick still cried, and Patty tried to deal with her own feelings. The hardest thing for her was watching her children struggle.

Patty finally brought Caitlyn and Patrick to a counseling group for children dealing with death, and after a few sessions she witnessed a big change in Caitlyn. Caitlyn begin to see that there were other children without dads, and many of them felt the same as she did. Once Caitlyn came to the realization that her dad was physically gone, Patty was able to talk to her about her spiritual beliefs. The family learned to understand that visits from butterflies were Daddy saying, "Hello." Butterflies would land on the children's noses, just where Daddy used to give them a gentle kiss. Pennies would be found in the house in places where they knew they did not put them, and they realized that pennies do come from heaven.

In the evening as Patty tucks her children into bed, there are still times when Patrick will sob, "Mommy, I miss Daddy," but now Caitlyn will say, "Mommy, I miss him, too," and together they hug.

While I was doing a workshop, I met Kelly who had just lost her husband. Kelly was dealing with her own grief but was very concerned about her twelve-year-old daughter, Kim. Her father had a long battle with cancer, and Kim never accepted that her dad was going to die. When her father finally did pass into spirit, he left both Kim and her mom profoundly grief stricken.

Kim's mom reached out for help by working with me as well as with a grief counselor. She began to deal with the pain she felt inside, but Kim could not come to terms with her loss. The more her mother tried to make her communicate her feelings, the more she shut down. She even started to rebel. Kim loved her dad very much, and her bond with him was even stronger than with her mother. She felt abandoned, afraid and angry. There were times she wished her mother had died and not her father, and these thoughts weighed her down with guilt.

In my experience with grieving families, I find that these thoughts and feelings are common in children as they process a great loss. Kim wanted to be strong for her mother, but at times being around her mother reminded her of her father. It was much easier to push her feelings down and live on the surface. During our session, Kim's father came to her and told her how much he loves her. He told me to tell her that it does not matter how much she rebels because her foundation is strong, and she will eventually find balance. She is a good girl, and that will always shine through. He also confirmed that he does visit with her, something she suspected every time she found a shiny penny in her room. As she stared at me with her sad blue eyes, not a tear fell. She asked me to tell other parents to give their children space, to not force questions on them because sometimes the answers aren't there yet. Kim wanted herself and other children to be given the freedom to grieve in their own time even if it may seem best to begin moving through all the stages immediately after the death. Please tell parents, Kim asked me, to remember that children have the right to choose how they want to walk their path. I was moved by Kim's concern for other children in pain and felt blessed to have met her.

Tony is a client who called me because he was having visitations in his home. His two-year-old child was communicating with spirits, and this made Tony very uncomfortable. He told a friend at work about the situation, and she gave him my number. I explained to Tony that ghostbusting is not my line of work but that perhaps I could communicate with one of his relatives who is in spirit and find some answers for him there. He agreed.

I soon discovered that Tony had never been allowed to grieve death as a child, so when I opened for our session, many spirits came through. When the spirit of his father came to me, I felt pressure in my chest and the sense of a quick death. I also saw him as a balding young man. Tony confirmed that this was his father. Then a strong smell of cigars came to me. I asked who that might be. Tony said it was his father who had a cigar and pipe collection.

Tony's father told me he was very proud of his son. He was sorry he did not have the opportunity to be with him as he grew but was very happy that Tony has this special time with his own son. He told him to appreciate this time and enjoy his son's childhood. He also told Tony that his health would fail if he didn't make some changes.

"Now he is talking about a ball," I said. "I think it is a ball he bought for you," I explained. Tony then told me that just before his father's chest pain began, they were playing football together with the ball he had bought for him. "Your father is now telling me that he is sorry about your mother," I said. "Do you understand what he means by that?"

"Yes," Tony said, "I don't speak to her. We just don't get along."

"Your father wants you to make peace with her. He is telling me she had a hard life. He knows she has a sharp tongue, but she is still your mother. Just love her unconditionally. He also wants to thank your son for seeing him and giving him the opportunity to talk to you."

Tony broke down in tears and shared his story. His father died when he was ten, and at the funeral his family told him not to cry. He had to be the man now and be strong for his family, they said. This responsibility was entirely unrealistic and inappropriate, yet many families tell the oldest child to take on the role the parent once had. As a result Tony closed down his grieving process. Now, thirty years later, he could finally grieve.

Parents, observe your children. Each is an individual and will need to grieve in different ways. Allow them their space but be there when they are ready for your help. You are their most important teacher, and you need to believe a concept before you can teach it to them. As you begin to understand the freedom that death brings, share this with your children. They are a lot more accepting of death than we realize. One way to approach the situation of death is to explain what happens to the soul after the physical body dies. The best time to do this is before a death occurs as it will be less stressful if you explain it with logic instead of emotion. The time to explain should not be while family members are grieving. It is difficult to try to assure them that everything is all right when your heart is breaking. Children are very advanced and can sense your energy field and even your most repressed emotions.

Different ethnic groups deal with grief in various ways, and grief was always expressed openly in my Catholic Italian family. In my case I was taken to viewings at a very early age but never told what was happening. When I watched my mother grieve for my brother, Neil, I thought death was a bad thing. She kept telling me that it was okay and that Neil was in heaven, but her sadness contradicted her words. I began telling my own daughter, Sarah, about heaven at an early age. I told her that the heavenly realm is a place far, far away, off in the sky. It is a place where spirits and angels play and a home for all spirits, even those of animals. I explained that this is where we all wait for a physical body. When we find the body we need, as well as the right Mommy and Daddy, we are born on Earth. We stay on Earth for a while, and then we go back home to heaven. I read her books about heaven so that when someone died, she would be able to picture a place where he went. Some of the books I particularly recommend are *The Next Place* by Warren Hanson and *What's Heaven?* by Maria Shriver. These books work for all types of families because they have no religious content but simply describe a place. You can teach your children your belief systems through these books or others like them. Then, when a death happens in your family, your children will be able to visualize a place where their loved one is dwelling.

When Sarah was three, my uncle Joe died. Lucas, Sarah and I attended his viewing. I took Sarah up to the casket and explained why Uncle Joe was in that "box," as she called it. I told her, "We are all gathered here to give thanks to Uncle Joe's body. His body allowed his soul to live in it for many years. When his body was not able to live anymore, his soul left. Without his soul, his body died." I pointed to his body, "You see, it is just an empty shell. It has no life without the soul inside." Then she asked me, "Where is the soul?" I told her, "It lives in the heavenly realm. Sometimes it comes down to Earth to visit." She asked me if it would be able to go back into his body. I told her, "No, once it leaves, it is very happy in heaven. Let's look around the room to see if we can see his soul visiting with us now." She asked me, "What does a soul took like?" I told her it could be a flash of light, a white mist floating in the room or just a warm feeling of love. She was excited and wanted to look for his soul right away. We did not see anything at that time, but later Sarah did tell me she saw spirits in our home. She was never afraid. A lot of children her age have nightmares, but Sarah never had one.

I had a client whose story is so heartbreaking that it will always stay in my memory. Her child was seven and had no concept of the other side. This little girl had a dream that two angels wanted her to go with them. She woke up from her dream very afraid, and her mother also became fearful. The child wanted to know more about the angels and where the angels wanted her to go. Her mother told her not to worry and dismissed the dream at once. Three months later, the child was involved in an accident and killed suddenly. Her mother's heart was filled with tremendous sorrow, but she also drew comfort from knowing that her child was with the angels who had come to her.

I believe it is very important to address your children's questions rather than brush them aside. In most cases children up to about age five still have access to memories of the heavenly realm, and thoughts of the other side are very wonderful for them. Older children should be given the opportunity to ask questions and to be taken seriously on the subject which will help eliminate the fear of death. Some children are very accepting of death, especially the youngest because they are still quite connected with the other side.

Tammy was a young woman in her late twenties. She called me to contact her sister. During the session her sister's spirit came through to me, and I felt as if I couldn't breath. I also sensed that she carried a fear of death before she died, that she died quickly and that she was very young. I asked Tammy if her sister had an accident. She told me that Doreen drowned at the age of four.

Doreen's spirit asked me to ask Tammy if she remembered her visits when she was a child. Tammy was silent for a moment.

"Yes, I sort of remember," she said.

Then the spirit of her sister asked, "Do you remember the games we used to play?"

"Tell her I don't remember the games," said Tammy, "but my mother told me I used to play hide and seek with her. I was two when she died and have very little memory of her death."

Tammy later explained that her mother told her she would be able to talk to her sister even though she had died. I asked her if she grieved after Doreen's death, and she replied that she hadn't because she felt as if her sister never left. Years later, her mother told her that she had heard Tammy playing and conversing with her sister but thought she was in denial and pretending to have a playmate. When her mother asked Tammy who she was talking to, the girl said, "It's Doreen." This upset her mother even though she believed in the afterlife and had even told her surviving daughter that communication would be possible.

Tammy realized that her behavior hurt her mother, and she stopped talking to Doreen. Part of her still thought she had been a crazy little girl for talking to her dead sister, but after our session she realized that she and Doreen have always been together. Their eternal bond of love is natural and a wonderful gift.

Justin is an eight-year-old boy with much knowledge of the other side, and meeting him was a privilege for me. He explained that he was suffering with the life-threatening disease of Klippel Trenaunay Weber Syndrome and had already had fifteen surgeries in his young lifetime. As we spoke, Justin told me that when he heard that his Pop Pop was very sick, he went into his room and said to himself, "Oh, man, Pop Pop might die." He wanted to focus on the positive, so he pulled out a notebook and started to write about all the things he and his Pop Pop did together and all the times they laughed together. "I didn't want to lose the memories," he told me. After his grandfather died, Justin went to the viewing and cried and cried. "I felt angry that I couldn't play with him anymore and that my little brother would never have the memories that I have," he said.

Three days after Pop Pop's death, Justin's other grandfather took him on a fishing trip to a cabin. While Justin and his grandfather were fishing, his grandfather became angry with him for not listening. Justin ran off to be by himself. He sat on a rock by the water. When he looked into the water, he saw the reflection of Pop Pop's face looking at him. He looked over his shoulder, but no one was there. He felt the loving presence of his Pop Pop and knew that he was all right. That night before he went to sleep, he saw another comforting vision of his Pop Pop. He told me his Pop Pop had little angel wings and was with another man. When he told his mother about his vision, she showed him the family photo album. Justin recognized the man he had seen in his vision to be his great uncle who had died sixteen years earlier.

Riding a bicycle was hard for Justin because of his disease. One day, as he was struggling to pedal his bike, he started to fall. He told me that he felt someone stop the bike from falling and set it in an upright position. "I knew it was my Pop Pop standing behind me."

Justin told me that he didn't feel different from other children. He said many of them have visions too. "We can talk to each other about it, but most kids don't feel comfortable talking to adults." He added, "Grown-ups are afraid of these things."

He knows that his chances of dying at a young age are very real, and he doesn't worry. I feel the reason he is not afraid to die is because he has never lost the closeness with those on the other side. However, he fights to stay alive because he sees sadness in his mother's eyes.

CHAPTER 12

Connecting with Your Loved One

We rely on our five senses from the time of our birth. Studies have shown that babies who are not held have little chance to survive. Touching, holding and simply feeling the presence of those we love is a vital part of life. You may experience an overwhelming sense of sadness as you dwell on the thought of not being able to feel the arms of your spouse around you. You may long to brush away a tear from a child's cheek or hear his voice calling to you. The physical senses we used to relate to our loved ones on Earth are now gone, but your bond of love will survive in another way. You can now experience your blessed relationship on a soul level. The relationship between two souls starts long before your birth on Earth. It is infinite, going on through time.

As you read this chapter, you will be able to go deep within yourself to feel the union that you had with your loved one—not the pain of the death but the bond that was there before the death. That connection is eternal. You will be able to go to the vision of light that lives deep within you. That is your soul, the place where the eternal link still lives. The tie is still inside your loved one's soul, and it is that which connects you.

For example, when a spouse dies, his partner may remarry because there is now a need for a physical relationship. Even though she marries again, the union that she once shared with her departed spouse is still there. It is now on a soul level. I am often asked by clients, "What happens if I marry again? Will I have two spouses when I go to the other side?" I always answer, "When a soul progresses on the other side, there is no ownership or labeling such as 'husband' or 'wife.' There is only unconditional love with no ego. The souls are together as part of a picture that is bigger than we can perceive here."

Clearly, a soul can have many different interconnections. The fulfillment and love that was shared in the first marriage is completely different in the second. The soul has a different purpose in each. Sit quietly for a few moments. Focus on your breath. Feel your breath moving in and out of your body. Pull your focus deep within your solar plexus. Keep breathing until you can feel this life within you. Feel the vibration of life deep within your gut. Feel the sensation that is alive within you. This is your first connection. This joining together with yourself has to come first. When you can understand what this feels like, you can connect with your loved one. This is the first step for the new relationship with your loved one. Once you remove your thoughts from your physical body and connect with your soul, communication will happen.

Your thoughts are a very important part of this new relationship. After our loved ones are on the other side, we tend to still talk to them. They can hear us, but occasionally they may not understand. Therefore, the topics we speak of must change. Earlier, we explored the soul's progression. When our loved one has advanced into a group soul, his memories of the details on Earth are gone, but the love you shared is as strong as ever. Thoughts of materialism, worries and fears that are a part of our everyday life are not relevant to one who is now in spirit. Not that the spirit doesn't care, it just cannot relate to our material world.

Marion, who is in her seventies, lost her husband eight years ago. She came to me for guidance because she was distraught about the home she and her husband had shared. She had not been able to keep up with repairs, and the house was in poor condition. As I opened up, I felt the warmth of love surround her. I said, "There is a man who is slightly balding. He tells me that he loved to wear knitted vests. He says he was your husband."

Tears immediately filled Marion's eyes as she exclaimed, "Yes, yes. You've reached my husband!" I felt five sharp pains in my heart and told Marion. She said, "You're right. My husband had five heart attacks before he went into spirit."

I said, "He is telling you that his love continues."

Marion replied, "Yes, my darling, and I love you. I have problems with the house, and I don't know where to turn. You have to help me." I told her there was no answer from him. Marion was quite agitated, and her voice grew louder "Who should I get to fix the roof?" Her husband was silent. "The roof leaks. Help me fix it!" she demanded.

Her husband finally said, "It will be all right. I love you."

I tried to explain to Marion that his connection with material things was gone. I said it is good that he has lost the worries of the Earth plane. His spirit is progressing. She looked at me in confusion as she was so absorbed in her material life that she could not grasp what I was saying. When Marion calmed down, I told her that there is a new language that the spirits speak, and it is about freedom. They feel freedom from all worries and fears that we have surrounding our lives on Earth. They are very excited about their newfound liberty and want to share it with us. We can feel this freedom when we talk to them and start to use their language.

A good way to start leaving materialistic thoughts out of our conversations is to read to our loved ones.

Pick a book or poem that speaks of the soul. The spirits love when you read to them. It becomes a special time for both of you. They listen to the sound of your voice, and you can take comfort in the fact that you are bringing them pleasure. When you pick material that pertains to the growth of the soul, it becomes an endless learning experience. *Emmanuel's Book* by Pat Rodegast and Judith Stanton is a great selection for your first attempts to communicate. You can ask the spirit to guide you to a page that contains material that it would like to discuss or bring to your attention.

Following is an exercise that will help you sense your loved one.

Go to a place where you feel close to your loved one. Make yourself comfortable and close your eyes. Picture a white light around you. Focus on your breath, breathing in and breathing out and thinking of nothing but the sound and sensations of your breath. After several minutes of focusing on your breathing, start to think loving thoughts of the spirit with whom you wish to communicate. Keep material thoughts out of your mind by sending your love for the soul out into the universe. Feel the love of your souls fuse together.

Allow your senses to be aware of the room around you. Be still and focus on your breath. You will start to feel warmth as your loved one comes into your energy field. This is a spiritual hug. You may feel a tingle on the top of your head or pressure on the back of your neck. This is the spirit touching you. The hair may stand up on your arms as the spirit brushes against you, or you may just experience a feeling of overall comfort. One of my clients felt her husband rubbing her cheek as the tingling sensation ran up and down her face. Give yourself an estimated time of twenty minutes before you gently open your eyes. Remember to trust your feelings. Know that whatever love you shared with your loved one when he was in the physical body will not leave just because the body is gone. You and that soul still share the love you once had, but now you are developing a new relationship. Trust what you just felt.

Tom is a man who feels a strong connection with his wife who has been in spirit for two years. When he came to me for a reading, he expressed the need to build a new relationship with his wife. I gave him the preceding exercise to do, and to his surprise he said goodbye to his old relationship. He cleared his mind and began a new bond. Tom told me, "I sat in her favorite chair, closed my eyes and began the meditation to communicate with my wife. I felt her eagerness to be in contact with me immediately. I felt a sensation through my hair. I could actually feel it move. I could smell her. It was so overwhelming that I had to stop.

"The next day I started again, and I could feel the same sensation in my hair. This time I heard her voice, and she told me she was sorry. I knew exactly what she was talking about. We were able to put closure on the old relationship and start on a new one."

One of my clients, Judith, had been doing meditations for years. It was quite easy for Judith to enter into the meditation, and she contacted her father the first morning she tried. She told me, "I heard my father say 'good morning.' I could sense him around me. He told me what he was doing on the other side. I was able to ask him questions, and we resolved issues from my childhood."

It may be difficult to focus at first; your mind may wander. Keep trying and your mind will get accustomed to meditation after a few tries. Once you make your first connection, the exercise will become easier. I created these meditations to help you focus and release material thoughts from your mind. The meditations are words that your loved ones can understand. Read them over and pick one for this day. Get comfortable and focus on your breath. Breathing in, breathing out. Read the meditation over and over to your loved one. Read it aloud or to yourself, whichever is more comfortable for you. Then sit quietly and feel the connection. Trust in what you feel.

Meditation 1

May the love in my heart reach your soul.
May the warmth of my love shine to your spirit.
Now I feel you near,
Thinking spiritual thoughts with you,
Feeling universal love in you,
Merging in spirit through you.
This experience with you is a true connection.

Meditation 2

I send my love to you
In the spiritual realm,
So my seeking soul will find you.
When I think of you with spiritual thoughts
In this way, we shall be united.

Meditation 3

In the light of universal thoughts,
Our souls blend.
Through these thoughts,
together we shall grow.

Meditation 4

Our souls are bound together.
I send our faithful love
Into the fields of spirit.
If you turn to me from the heavens where spirits dwell,
You will find me thinking of love.

Eileen told me a story about her brother who passed rather suddenly. They had been good friends, and Eileen missed their camaraderie and his sense of humor. He died before she had a chance to say goodbye, and Eileen decided that she wanted to start a new bond with him. She began with "Meditation 3". Eileen said, "I sat down quietly to begin my meditation. My left side became very warm, and my hair felt as if someone was moving a hand through it. I began to smile."

She paused for a moment, then continued. "I was holding a crystal in both of my hands. I felt two hands cup mine and hold them. I could feel my brother." The next day she tried again but did not receive any messages. She tried again the following day as she sat in her office listening to music. Eileen said, "I read the poem. As I was reading, I felt immense heat move down my left side and again felt the sensation in my hair. I saw my brother in my mind's eye, and he was smiling at me. I am so excited. I can actually feel my brother's presence."

When Patty and Bob vowed "until death do us part" on their wedding day, Patty never imagined their life together would actually end. After nineteen years of marriage, Bob was diagnosed with cancer. His fight for survival intensified their love. He eventually lost the fight, and Patty had to learn to start her life over. She was overwhelmed with sadness and anger.

At the time Patty took my workshop, she was still very connected to Bob. When she did the meditations, he was by her side. In the quiet space of her home, Patty sat and read "Meditation 2". She immediately felt Bob enter her energy field. Tingling went through her head and neck and spread down her body, and she suddenly felt heavy and very drowsy. The next thing she knew, she was aware of being asleep and heard voices. When she woke up, she could still feel the tingling throughout her body. Her hands felt warm as if Bob were holding them. The tingling became even stronger. She felt as if love from Bob was being sent to her, so she projected love back to him. She closed her eyes and felt the warmth of his love and pictured him and sent love back to him. Her lips started to tingle, and she knew Bob was kissing her.

Patty told me that doing this meditation made it much easier to contact Bob because it gave her something to concentrate on rather than just thinking about him and becoming sad. Focusing on the meditation allowed her to communicate with him in the here and now without reminiscing. Patty is now trying to move on with her life, but she knows that whenever she needs to feel Bob's love, she can go into meditation and experience the bond that always exists between them.

Bridget lost her son David in a car accident fourteen months before I met her. She attended a workshop to help process her grief. She was told her sadness would disappear after a year, and when it didn't, she began to suffer from anxiety attacks. Bridget was caught in the depression stage of grief, and she knew she had to do something to help herself.

After attending the workshop a second time, she felt as if she had regained some control over her life. She worked very hard to come to the stage of acceptance and was ready to start a new relationship with her departed son. If she allowed herself to think about David, she would slip into depression, but when she focused on a meditation, she entered a new, healing space. She repeated "Meditation 4" at night before going to sleep, and after a few months, Bridget started to feel a presence near her. Several days later, she felt tingling all over her body, then fell asleep. During her sleep she knew she had had a visitation from David.

Eventually, she would do the meditation and awaken after several hours with a message from David. One time, he told her to take care of Dad and stop fighting with him. A week later, she learned her husband had developed dangerously high blood pressure. Bridget now cherishes her new bond of love with David.

Mary's father owned his own business which was attached to the house, and she grew up with him around the house throughout the day. She loved to spend time with him. She enjoyed helping him any way she could from the time she was very young until he died.

After a session with me, Mary found complete validation in what her father told me. She was convinced I was going to help her on her path. She chose "Meditation 1" and diligently read it every night for several weeks. One night while doing her meditation, she felt an incredible wave of love wash over her body. As she sat in this feeling of love, she heard the word "love" being repeated inside her head. She then felt her father's presence and knew she had connected with him. When Mary opened her eyes, she saw a vision of her father standing in the doorway. Within seconds he disappeared, but she knew he was watching her meditate. Then inside her head, she heard him say, "Bits, just checkin' in on you." Since that time, Mary has had many similar visits with her father. She finds comfort in knowing she has built a new relationship with him.

When I met Debbi, her pain was extremely intense. Her husband had been in spirit for four months, and she did not know how she was going to continue living. Debbi studied with me and after three months had said her goodbye to the old relationship. Debbi was aware that she and her husband were soul mates, so they were able to join together in a new relationship. Debbi told me that when she meditates, she always feels him touching her hair and back of her neck. "Once he even tickled my nose," she said. "I started to read 'Meditation 1,' and after a few lines I told him how much I missed what we had. I know we will never be able to have that again."

Debbi took a deep breath and went on, "He told me, 'What we will have when we are together again without our earthly binding will be even better.'" Debbi said, "I felt a lot of energy around and in my hair. I asked him if he was trying to mess it up. Then I felt him laughing. All of a sudden, I felt as if we were dancing. I could smell him and feel his arms around me."

Debbi's new relationship had begun. When you start to communicate with the spirits on a soul level, you will feel them. The spirit will listen to your words. The words will no longer come from your thoughts; they will emerge from your soul. The connection will be made. The new bond will grow deeper. Trust it.

CHAPTER 13

Communicating Through Meditations

Prayer is talking. Meditation is listening. Sitting in silence is very important in our lives whether you are meditating for communication or just seeking peace within yourself. It is a wonderful habit which enhances your life, a form of mental exercise that will take you into other dimensions. It will raise your vibrations and allow you to experience other realms. Meditation also has therapeutic effects such as developing breath control which strengthens the energy flow of your body. This natural healing restores power to your body and can improve your immune system for overall health and clarity of thought. Meditation affects the memory centers of your brain and helps improve the decision-making process. It may also relieve any unpleasant mental state of your mind or body.

A simple daily meditation can have an enormous impact on the grief process. As you let yourself relax, you enter into the state of nothingness where communication takes place. This is the Alpha level of the mind frequency. In this chapter we will explore more direct ways of communicating with the other side.

Before you contact a spirit, you must first prepare yourself for meditation. To do this, you must find a comfortable place where you will not be disturbed. Address your God power, a higher power from your belief system with whom you feel secure. I use Jesus the Christ. Before any meditation, you must always call on your God power and wrap white light around you. This insures you that only spirits from the highest realm will come to you. The information from those of the higher realm will be given with love and understanding. It is always positive.

Sit in a chair or lie propped up with several pillows. It's best to not lie completely flat because you may fall asleep. Soft, soothing music is an option, but you can also meditate in silence.

White Light Meditation

Close your eyes. Take a deep breath, hold to the count of three and relax. Take another deep breath and hold to the count of three and relax. Repeat one more time. Sit still for a few moments and focus on your breath going in your nose and down into your lungs, filling your lungs and then flowing out of your mouth. See white light coming down from the heavens through the roof, through the ceiling, and gently into the top of your head. Feel the warmth as the light enters your head. It is relaxing your eyes, your nose and your mouth. Feel the white light going into your cheeks and down to your jaw. As you start to relax, allow your jaw to gently hang open. Feel the white light going down your neck, massaging your shoulders. Now it travels down your arms and into your hands. Feel the warmth in your hands as the white light goes through your fingers. Now feel it in your chest, feel the warmth moving from your chest into your abdomen and into your pelvic area. It continues down your thighs, your knees and through your feet. Be aware of the white light going into the floor and deep into Mother Earth. You are now one with Father Sky and Mother Earth. You are one with the universe. Feel the white light wrap around you clockwise as it wraps you in a cocoon. Feel the warmth as it surrounds you. Feel the love as you now sit in your white light meditation. Spend a few minutes there, focusing on your breath. Now slowly bring yourself back. Feel the white light moving counterclockwise as it unwraps. Move your fingers one by one. Feel the room around you. Slowly open your eyes. You will feel deeply relaxed, at peace and grateful for the loving universe that surrounds you at all times.

Another meditation I use frequently is the "Meditation for Communication." I love this meditation and have shared it with many clients who have found great benefit from it. It is important to keep an open mind when doing the "Meditation for Communication." Do not call any particular loved one because the one who needs to be there will come to you. If it is not the one you hoped for, be patient

    Joni is a young lady who came to me longing to see her boyfriend again. He had died suddenly before she had a chance to say goodbye. Joni wanted to learn how to have a new relationship with him, so I taught her the "Meditation for Communication." Joni's boyfriend did not come the first time she did this exercise, but her father did. Joni did not have a good relationship with her father, and she was very upset. She wanted to stop the meditation, but I asked her to please continue. Joni's father told her how sorry he was for the things he did to her. He eased the pain in her heart by telling her that there was something wrong with him, and she was blameless. The communication had stopped, and Joni was sobbing, but I could see that her father's spirit was still there. He appeared to me as a tall man in his sixties. He looked worn, and I could feel the sensation of alcohol, telling me that he had a drinking problem. When I described him, Joni answered through her sobs to confirm that it was her father. He repeated his message to me in order to be sure that Joni knew of his regrets. He wanted me to tell her that he felt the pain he had inflicted on her when he went through his soul review. He asked me to ask her to please forgive him and to forgive herself as she was not at fault in any way. She had been a child when he abused her.

When I told Joni what her father had asked, she said, "I'm so happy you made me continue with the meditation." She wiped the tears from her cheeks, took a deep breath and continued, "I've held on to this pain for years, and it has been unbearable at times. Now that he has admitted what he did, I can move on with my life. I can't tell you what a relief this is for me." Joni's boyfriend came to her in subsequent sessions, and their souls started their new relationship. Her father never returned.

Meditation for Communication

Close your eyes. Take a deep breath, hold to the count of three and relax. Take another deep breath and hold to the count of three and relax. Repeat one more time. Sit still for a few moments and focus on your breath going in your nose and down into your lungs, filling your lungs and then flowing out of your mouth. See white light coming down from the heavens through the roof, through the ceiling, and gently into the top of your head. Feel the warmth as the light enters your head. It is relaxing your eyes, your nose and your mouth. Feel the white light going into your cheeks and down to your jaw. As you start to relax, allow your jaw to gently hang open. Feel the white light going down your neck, massaging your shoulders. Now it travels down your arms and into your hands. Feel the warmth in your hands as the white light goes through your fingers.

Now feel it in your chest, feel the warmth moving from your chest into your abdomen and into your pelvic area. It continues down your thighs, your knees and through your feet. Be aware of the white light going into the floor and deep into Mother Earth. You are now one with Father Sky and Mother Earth. You are one with the universe. Feel the white light wrap around you clockwise as it wraps you in a cocoon. Remain in the cocoon and imagine yourself floating. Let go of your body completely and imagine the floor giving way beneath you, leaving you afloat in the universe. Envision a field of beautiful grass. Walk toward the grass and feel the soft, cool blades beneath your feet as you walk upon it. Feel the longer blades brush against your ankles. Feel the warmth of the sun on your face and the fresh breeze dancing through your hair. Walk through the field to the other side where there is a park lined by many trees. See the bench at the far end of the park. Walk slowly to the bench and sit down at one end. Look into the distance which is full of white mist. Stare into the white mist. As you stare, you can see someone standing in the mist. It is the spirit of one of your loved ones who is now walking out of the mist and coming toward you. The spirit approaches and sits at the other end of the bench. You can feel the love of this spirit flowing toward you. Slowly count to three and on the third count, ask the spirit to tell you his or her name. If you do not hear the name, count to three again and repeat the question. Sit with the spirit for a few minutes and receive the message of love to be shared with you. It is time to go back. The spirit returns into the mist. This is not "goodbye" but "until the next time." Get up from the bench and slowly walk through the park, through the field and into your cocoon of light. It gently unwraps from around you. You are safe. You are home. Slowly open your eyes.

If you think that you have made contact, wonderful; you did. If you are not sure, believe that you have. Whether it was a feeling, a sound or a hazy picture in your head, trust it. If you feel that you did not make any contact, don't be discouraged. It may take more than one try. If you have not made contact after a few tries, you may need to continue working through your grief; there could be something that you have not yet released.

The next meditation is designed to help you understand what it feels like when the soul leaves the physical body. This knowledge creates the bond of understanding between your soul and the soul of your loved one. At times, the spirit will even take part in the meditation. You will learn that death is not a painful experience, but quite the contrary. All physical pain and all the sensations of the physical body leave at the moment of death. The spirit then takes over. I call this exercise the "Meditation on Transition."

Meditation on Transition

Sit quietly and focus on your breath. I am going to ask you to take three deep breaths at your own pace.

Please make sure you breathe deeply and slowly. Now breath normally. Feel your body getting heavier. As if you can almost feel the gravity, hold on to your body. Feel the denseness of your body as it is drawn to Earth. For a moment the senses of this heavy body become heightened. Feel the temperature in the room as it caresses your skin. Listen to how the smallest sounds become magnified. Be aware of the scents that surround you. For one last time your outer world becomes alive. Take a few minutes to allow yourself to experience this sensation. Now notice within this heavy body a glimmer of light. You may even sense a feeling of warmth. For a moment your body seems to come alive. Now, within the heavy body there is a body of awareness. Sense this light body. Experience its presence. As you focus on this light, you may even notice a sense of calmness. This place inside you may feel different from the physical body which is full of confusion, fear and maybe even anger. However, within this light deep within you, there is total tranquility. Allow yourself to become one with this calmness. But remember both of these bodies together create you, you who are named in this life. When the dense body dies, the light body becomes the eternal you who has no beginning and no end. Allow this glimmer of light within you to become stronger. Your consciousness is drawn to its radiance. See how each breath maintains that connection, allowing life to stay one more moment in the body. Feel the contact between the light body and the dense body that each breath provides. Feel how each breath sustains the light body balanced perfectly within you. Take each breath as though it were the last. Experience each inhalation as though it is not going to be followed by another. Gently, breath in and out. Let that last breath go, the last breath of life leaving the body behind, the connection severed between the light body and the heavy body. The final breath. Gently let it go. Trust the process. The last breath vanished into space. Leave your body where it lies and become this light body, your soul. There you are shining before an eternal light. Become one with your true self. Gently, allow yourself to float free out of the body. Enter the vastness of being. Enter into the light. Merge into the light, uniting with the absolute joy of your true nature, light merging with light. Let go of your name. Let go of your identity and float free in the vastness. As you become one with the light, you feel a sense of safely and comfort, so deep and natural. Float free in the light, in the joy, in the freedom of your soul. You may even feel the love and presence of your angels, spirit guides or a loved one. Sit several moments in silence to enjoy the sensation of being within the light. Now feel yourself coming back. You may even see your silver cord which is still attached to your body. Grab hold and bring yourself back. The light body settles again into the heavy body. Feel the reunion. Take a few moments to breathe gently. With each breath become aware of your physical body, allowing the two bodies to become one. Each breath will join your soul and your physical body together again on Earth, bringing with you a new birth into this world, a clearing and an understanding. May you feel peace and send this peace throughout the world. Focus on your breath. Inhale and exhale the air that is your life energy. Feel the white light unwrapping. Wiggle your fingers. Feel the chair beneath you. Slowly open your eyes.

Meditation is not something that comes naturally. It is a learned experience, but I feel it is vital in our lives. I suggest that you start with the "White Light Meditation" once a day. Sit in the meditation for about twenty minutes. This will help your mind get used to the stillness. When you are comfortable with the "White Light Meditation," do the "Meditation for Communication" once a week. The practice of meditation will become part of your life. I tell my students that if you can keep your mind quiet for three seconds in the beginning, you are doing very well. Some of my students had developed regular communication in six weeks; others practiced for months before having a visitation. It is important to get comfortable with meditating, and your new relationship with spirit will happen. Be patient. It will come at the right time. This practice will bring good benefits to every part of your life.

CHAPTER 14

Dream Visitations

The easiest way for spirit to communicate with you is in your dreams. A spirit may appear to you in what you think is a dream immediately after death. This is not a dream. This is the departing soul in its astral body stopping briefly to say goodbye before leaving the Earth plane. Many people have given accounts of having been contacted by spirits who had just died, sometimes before knowing of the person's death. Manuela's dream is an example.

As Manuela lay on her bed, drifting in and out of sleep, she felt someone walk through her room. She immediately thought of the name, "Eddie," who was her dear friend. As she remembered the vision the next day, she thought she might have been asleep during the experience. However, she learned later that Eddie had died at approximately the same time she had thought of his name. She realized that she had experienced a visitation rather than a dream.

My uncle Jimmy heard a sound at his window one morning. He knew there was a spirit waiting to come in, so he opened the window as a welcome. He said that Neil came in to his apartment for a short visit and then left. He did not learn of Neil's death until later that day. Sometimes the spirit may appear in a dream soon after death because you may be in a state of shock or denial. But if your state of denial changes to depression or anger, the spirit will step back and give you space to grieve. Be patient. The spirit will know when you are ready to be contacted. If you are not ready when you get your visitation in your dream, you may become anxious and hurry to bed each night to see your loved one, possibly losing the focus on your own life.

Your soul makes a choice to come into the body in order to learn its lessons and advance on its path. However, the soul cannot be housed in a body twenty-four hours a day because it is accustomed to being free. It will take any opportunity to return to its natural state. While you are asleep, you are giving your soul the opportunity to leave your body. It is still connected by a silver cord along which it is pulled back. For example, you may notice that sometimes when you awaken, you cannot move your hands or body. Your mind is awake, but your body will not move. Your soul has been traveling into other dimensions, places where your loved ones dwell, and when you pull it back, you automatically wake up. Your consciousness is back, but your physical body is not yet connected to it.

Dreams are often a source of comfort such as those in which Neil visited my mother and helped her find solace. Months had gone by after my brother's death, and Mom's agony was as painful as the day he died. She would throw herself on the bed sobbing and screaming, and no one could comfort her. She tossed and turned at night, unable to stay asleep for any length of time. One night, when she finally fell into a fitful sleep, she dreamed of Neil. He came to her room and told her, "Stop crying and take care of Dad. He needs you. I'm okay. It's just like being here." Then he said, "I have to go. Your friend Angie needs me." He seemed to drift out of the window. The dream continued, and my mother looked out the window and down the block. She could see an emergency vehicle and two stretchers. Neil took one stretcher and left. The next morning, Mom learned that her friend Angie and her husband had been in an automobile accident, and Angie had died. My mother was comforted because she knew Neil was with God and had a job on the other side.

Later Mom had surgery and needed routine visits to the doctor for follow-up. One night before a visit, she had another dream about Neil. He told her to tell the boatman that it was okay. My mother did not understand the message but tucked it away in her mind. There were a few people sitting in the doctor's waiting room when my mother signed in and sat down. One man looked at her for a few minutes and then came to the empty chair next to her and sat down. He introduced himself as the man who sold the boat to Neil before the accident. He told my mother how sorry he was for her loss and said he had tried to talk Neil out of buying that particular boat because someone else had been thrown from it. However, Neil wanted that boat, and he would not listen. The man had felt guilt since the accident. The dream was vivid in my mother's mind, and she was able to help the man by telling him that she knew Neil's strong personality and did not blame him for the accident. By coming to his mother in a dream, Neil was able to bring emotional healing to another person.

When I started working in the clubs in New York, I met Fran. We became best friends and shopped together, had meals together and even traveled abroad together. She finally met the man she thought was the love of her life, but he turned out to be a big disappointment and finally left her. She was devastated and angry for a long time but then returned to her positive way of thinking. She once again began to search for the right man as she desperately wanted to have a family.

Fran suddenly discovered that she had ovarian cancer which ended her dream of having a family. Her chemotherapy treatments made her quite ill, and I spent as much time with her as I could. I always thought that there was nothing we would not do for each other, and I helped her when she was weak from her treatments.

Fran survived her first bout with cancer as well as the second one seven years later. A few years after that, the cancer attacked her liver, and her condition became serious. I had moved to a different state and had a small child, so we had only been able to communicate with each other by phone for some time.

One day a mutual friend called to tell me that I had to visit Fran as soon as possible if I wanted to see her while she was still alive. I couldn't bear the thought of seeing Fran in such a condition. She was my dearest friend and had been so full of life that I just couldn't imagine her frail figure in a wheelchair. In addition, our lives had taken different paths since my spiritual awakening. She did not believe in life after death, so I agonized over how we should discuss her passing away.

I found my courage and decided to visit Fran at her sister's home in New Jersey. Fran was anxious to see the baby, so I decided to take Sarah along. Fran was hospitalized before I was able to visit. I planned to see her as soon as she was released, but she died three days later. I felt so remorseful that I couldn't bear to contact her spirit even though I felt her presence and knew she wished to communicate with me. One night before going to sleep, I asked Fran to come to me in a dream. I wanted to tell her that I was sorry that I was not there for her at the end.

During the night I dreamed that Fran pulled up beside me in a limousine. As she rolled down the car window, I saw that she looked very tired. I apologized for being unable to see her before she died. She said,

"It's just like being on the Earth plane. There is a lot of work to do on one's self." I saw trees and a sunset. I asked if she was in the heavenly realm. She said, "Sort of. When I first died, I went there. Now I am in a dimension that is like Earth. I am still attached to the Earth plane, so I came to this place of learning. I will return to the heavenly realm when I have learned what I need to know."

I asked if she was angry with me. She said, "Not anymore; I understand now." I asked if she had gone to the light. "Yes," she answered. "I saw light all around me, and I felt myself getting lighter." I started to cry and said, "I love you." She told me that she loved me too. It was a poignant goodbye for both of us.

Sometimes validating communication is difficult because you had many dreams throughout the night, and by the time you awaken, your visitation is jumbled with other dreams. Therefore, you cannot always accept the dream as completely accurate. A visitation can usually be distinguished from a dream because it feels more intense than a typical dream. Try to sort out the different aspects of the dream and then piece them together to understand what appears relevant to you. The spirit will frequently appear in familiar surroundings such as the home where you grew up. My father usually appears in my dreams in the house we lived in together. This is a place to which we both can relate.

Karen is a woman who never thought much about life after death. One day as we were talking, she expressed an interest in communicating with her paternal grandfather. She had dreamt of him several times in the past and wished to dream of him again. She practiced some dream recall exercises but was frustrated when her attempts were unsuccessful. Therefore, she appealed to her deceased loved ones to see if anyone wished to communicate with her. Soon her great-grandmother appeared to her in a dream. Karen was very surprised that the dream took place in her paternal grandfather's house which her maternal great-grandmother had never even entered. It was a house in which Karen had felt very comfortable during many childhood visits. She dreamed that they sat together in the kitchen, and her great-grandmother told her not to worry because everything was okay. Karen noticed that, although there were many people and other events occurring in the dream, the main focus was the conversation with her great-grandmother. The part of the dream with her great-grandmother felt more like a visitation.

At the time the dream occurred, Karen was very frustrated because she and her husband lived with their two children in a crowded place. Soon after the dream, they were able to move into their own home.

Here are some techniques that may help you receive visitations from loved ones in your dreams:

- Go to bed earlier before you get too tired. Have "alone time" in your bed. This will help you ease into the dream state and have better recall.

- Say a prayer and do a meditation before sleep to ask the loved one to communicate with you in the dream state. When you lie down in your bed, picture a white light coming down from heaven, surrounding you. For example, I would say, "Neil, please come to me in my dreams to comfort me. As I sleep tonight, I ask my higher power to protect me and keep my dreams in the highest possible positive form." Ask the loved one you want to contact to come to you, but know that the spirit may not be able to come to you at that time. Be patient and know your loved one is with you, and you will eventually recall their visits.
- Keep a dream journal. In the morning as soon as you awake, write down the dream you had just before waking.
- If you want to remember dreams that you have throughout the night, drink water before going to bed so that your body will gently waken to go to the bathroom. Write in your dream journal at this time; otherwise you will forget. Do not use an alarm clock which shocks the body, making it feel paralyzed for a split second as the soul is jerked back into the body.

Do not become discouraged if you don't have dreams of your loved one right away. If you do the meditations and the journal writing, contact with your loved one will eventually be made.

CHAPTER 15

My Second Chance to Say Goodbye

I thought a lot about my own immortality while writing this book. Early one morning, while on a treadmill in a gym, I watched the clock as the minutes counted down. I was anxious for my twenty minutes to be up so I could get on with my day. Then I realized my life was counting down. I did not want to be in such a rush for my days to finish. I knew I wanted to tell you, my readers, to stop and live each day to the fullest. Have love for yourself and for anyone else you come into contact with during your day. We are all here for our own soul's purpose. We must dig deep inside ourselves and find this purpose. Being an example of a soul on a path is one way to help others to fulfill their own path. We are not here to worry about tomorrow. It will come before we know it, and soon we will find ourselves at our own soul review.

When I look back on my life, I see that I took a lot of detours as I traveled along my path. I am not proud of many of the choices I made, but those choices made me who I am today. I was once a young lady who did not stop to have compassion for others. I now live the life of a practicing Buddhist, and my life is all about compassion. My work with death has given me the lesson of life. When death is a major part of your life, you realize that you are not indestructible. I have learned to live each day as if it were my last. I know I have to do everything today instead of tomorrow. If you can live your life with that philosophy, worry and fear will disappear. As you stay in that precious moment, your path will unfold for you.

Saying goodbye is never easy. It is work. It involves making a drastic change and opening to a new life process. The one thing to remember is that even though you have to say goodbye to the relationship as you knew it, you are not saying goodbye to the spirit. This is what you really loved about the person. True, a change has happened in your life. You are now meeting your loved one in a different form. However, the bond between souls will always be there.

I do not hold emotional memories of the communication between spirits and my clients after my readings. Feeling the sadness of each story, day after day, would wreak havoc on my emotions, so the memory is taken away. When discussing the reading with the client after I come out of meditation, I have an objective relationship to the process and am not burdened with emotional energy that does not belong to me.

When writing this book, however, I felt the pain of my clients as I reflected on the work they had to do to start a new relationship with their loved ones. I came to realize that the circle of life is quite fragile.

As I sit on my chair and hold my two children on my lap, four year-old Sarah and sixteen-month-old Marcus, I have lovely memories. I remember the day the spirit of Sarah touched my hand and asked me to be born. I recall the visions of Marcus long before he was here. This was their souls building relationships with me long before they were in their physical bodies. These were bonds that we shared long before their births. I realize my body was only the vehicle for their souls to enter Earth. I am here to guide them and teach them morals and respect and hopefully instill in them my love for life. But beyond that, their souls need to be free to travel on their own paths.

When I look into my husband's eyes, I look deep into his soul. This is the relationship I want to know. When I speak to my mother, I hear the voice of her soul. When I hold my family, I look beyond the name. As I touch them, I touch their souls. I need to love them unconditionally. I need to build relationships with them on a soul level yet enjoy the funny, crazy things that they do.

I hope that I have conveyed in these pages the truth of my own experience that the bond our souls share is eternal. If you can accomplish this link while your loved one is alive, then the connection is no different when the physical body leaves. The voice of the soul remains. I know that for some this is hard to grasp, but isn't everything new a bit difficult? Every change that comes finds resistance at first.

Shortly before finishing this book I realized there was a goodbye I hadn't said. I had lost contact with Joey because of his drug and alcohol problems. He had also become very violent. Joey, who had been so important to me in my early years, who had told me that suicide is never the way out, committed suicide in 1985. No one told me of his death. My mother knew he had hung himself but didn't tell me until months later when she mentioned it in passing. I felt cheated of my chance to say goodbye or even to go to his funeral. I needed to have closure to a relationship that once meant so much to me. Feeling that need surprised me because, as a medium, I worked with others and their grief and rarely with my own. Now, all these years later, I had a dream. I saw Joey all dressed up and smiling. He looked healthy and happy, and his eyes sparkled. His eyes had been full of pain and darkness during his life. Thirteen years in the spirit world had washed the despair away, and now he was full of light. Joey was wearing a minister's collar, and I saw him in a church for spirits who had committed suicide. I knew this was symbolic. His soul had progressed and was now helping others who had taken their lives. He didn't speak, but he held me close. I felt closure.

When I woke, I felt a great sadness. At first, being separated from him again was overwhelming. Then the pain melted into pure love. I realized the hug we shared was my second chance to say goodbye.

About the Authors

Marianne Michaels is one of the nation's most respected and dedicated mediums. A pioneer in her field, she has helped people all across the country struggling with the death of someone close to them to rebuild their lives. Her landmark workshop, "A Second Chance To Say Goodbye: A Spiritual Journey," gives participants the emotional and spiritual support to work through their grief and the techniques to access and develop their own psychic ability to communicate with their loved ones.

Marianne's workshop is redefining the traditional role of the medium by giving friends and family members of those who have crossed over the opportunity for direct contact. A sought after speaker, Marianne lectures on life after death at churches, conferences, and seminars. She also works with the terminally ill and their families to prepare them spiritually. She provides them with peace and the understanding of the changes that will take place as death approaches and the soul transitions to the afterlife.

When she is not working, she enjoys her Siamese cat Miso and long walks in the beautiful Pennsylvania countryside with her dog Jacob. She has recently published her second book, *Healing the Heart of Grief: Stories of Hope from the Afterlife*.

Her websites are www.mariannemichaels.com and www.spiritualdying.com.

Anita Curtis, author of *Animal Wisdom: How to Hear the Animals*, has been working with animals for more than fifty years. Since childhood, Anita has had the ability to communicate with animals. Through training with Jeri Ryan, PhD, and advanced training with Penelope Smith, she has developed her animal communication abilities to a high degree.

Along with her private consultations, Curtis appears frequently on radio and television. She has been featured in magazine and newspaper articles throughout the country. She has recently published her second book, *Many Happy Returns: Reuniting with our Pets*.

Her website is www.anitacurtis.com.

Other Works by Marianne

If you have enjoyed this book, you might be interested in other offerings by Marianne. The following are available at www.mariannemichaels.com.

Readings

Individual Readings, In-Person and by Phone
Group Readings (Message Circles)
Call Marianne's office at 610-868-4017 for an appointment.

Books

Healing the Heart of Grief:
  Stories of Hope from the Afterlife

CDs and Digital Downloads

Healing the Heart of Grief
This CD features meditations used in the book, *Healing the Heart of Grief.*

A Second Chance to Say Goodbye
This CD features meditations used in the book, *A Second Chance to Say Goodbye.*

Transition: From the Way of the Soul
"Transition" will help you understand the love and peace your loved one felt when he or she crossed over.

Together Again: From the Way of the Soul
This CD answers many questions on what it is like on the other side, your divine plan and how souls travel together. It will reassure you that death is not the end of a relationship; that when someone you love dies, the two of you will find each other again whether in the heavenly realm or together again on Earth.

Angels: From the Way of the Soul
With this CD you will learn that your angels are with you at all times. It answers many questions on the subjects of angels and spirit guides and will help you meet your spiritual companions.